THE FOREIGN TEACHING ASSISTANT'S MANUAL

Patricia Byrd
Georgia State University

Janet C. Constantinides
University of Wyoming

Martha C. Pennington
University of Hawaii

COLLIER MACMILLAN

Library of Congress Cataloging-in-Publication Data

Byrd, Patricia.

    The foreign teaching assistant's manual / Patricia Byrd, Janet C. Constantinides, Martha C. Pennington.
       p.   cm.

    ISBN 0-02-317590-7

    1. Graduate teaching assistants—Training of—United States—Handbooks, manuals, etc. 2. Students, Foreign—United States—Handbooks, manuals, etc. 3. English language—United States—Study and teaching (Higher)—Foreign speakers—Handbooks, manuals, etc. 4. College teaching—United States—Handbooks, manuals, etc. I. Constantinides, Janet C. II. Pennington, Martha Carswell. III. Title.
LB2335.4.B97   1989
378'.122—dc19   87-38335
                                            CIP

Copyright © 1989 by Macmillan Publishing Company,
a division of Macmillan, Inc.

All rights reserved. No part of this book may be reproduced or transmitted in any form or by any means, electronic or mechanical, including photocopying, recording, or any information storage and retrieval system, without permission in writing from the Publisher.

Collier Macmillan Canada, Inc.

PHOTO CREDITS: Each part opens with a photo of a sculpture.
Part One: Auguste Rodin, French, 1840–1917. *The Thinker,* early 1880s. Bronze, dark brown patina on marble base. 78 x 51 x 52 3/4" (198 x 129.5 x 133.9 cm). Detail. By permission of The Fine Arts Museum of San Francisco. Gift of Alma de Bretteville Spreckels; Parts Two, Three, Four, and Five: Life-size bronze sculpture titled *Creating, Recess, Out to Lunch,* and *Spring* by J. Seward Johnson, Jr. Photos courtesy of Sculpture Placement, Ltd. of Washington, D.C.

Printing: 1 2 3 4 5 6 7   Year: 9 0 1 2 3 4 5

Collier Macmillan
ESL/EFL Department
866 Third Avenue
New York, NY 10022

Printed in the U.S.A.

ISBN 0-02-317590-7

Contents

Acknowledgments   vii
Introduction to the Instructor   ix
Introduction to the Teaching Assistant   xii

PART ◆ ONE

PREPARATORY ACTIVITIES

Chapter 1

Background to U.S. Education   3
● **Elementary and High School Education**
1.1   Background Assignment
1.2   Discussion Assignment
● **Organization of Higher Education**
1.3   Background Assignment
1.4   Discussion Assignment
● **Analysis of Faculty Roles and Behaviors**
1.5   Background Assignment
1.6   Discussion Assignment
● **Analysis of Student Roles and Behaviors**
1.7   Background Assignment
1.8   Discussion Assignment

Chapter 2

Departmental Relations   12
● **Organization of Departments**
2.1   Background Assignment
2.2   Directory of Your Department
● **Role of Graduate Teaching Assistants**
2.3   Background Assignment
2.4   Discussion Assignment

Chapter 3

Profiles of American Students   18
3.1   In the Classroom
    3.1.a   Preparing Before Class
    3.1.b   Asking Questions
    3.1.c   Discussing
    3.1.d   Challenging and Disputing
    3.1.e   Learning Styles
3.2   Outside the Classroom

    3.2.a   Asking for Help
    3.2.b   Questioning Grades
    3.2.c   Seeking Advice

Chapter 4

Profiles of Teachers in American Colleges and Universities   31
4.1   In the Classroom, Section 1
    4.1.a   Course Designer
    4.1.b   Lecturer
    4.1.c   Discussion Leader
    4.1.d   Review Session Leader
    4.1.e   Enforcer of Rules
    4.1.f   Textbook Adopter
4.2   In the Classroom, Section 2
    4.2.a   Dealing With Varieties of Students
    4.2.b   Teaching Styles
4.3   Outside the Classroom
    4.3.a   Conferences
    4.3.b   Office Hours
    4.3.c   Social Occasions

PART ◆ TWO

BACKGROUND TO TEACHING

Chapter 5

Planning and Organizing the Course   43
5.1   Setting Goals
5.2   Preparing the Course Syllabus

Chapter 6

Presenting in Class or Lab   46
6.1   Types of Explanations
6.2   More Work With Explanations
6.3   Characteristics of Effective Explainers
6.4   Organization of 50-Minute Classes
6.5   Adding Interest Through Associations, Examples, and Humor
6.6   Adding Variety to Class Formats

Contents

6.7 Nonverbal Communication
6.8 Asking and Answering Questions
6.9 A Reference Guide to Question Structures
6.10 A Reference Guide to Question Types

Chapter 7
Using Audiovisual Aids 64
7.1 The Chalkboard
7.2 The Overhead Projector
7.3 Other Types of Audiovisual Aids

Chapter 8
Leading a Discussion 70
8.1 Methods for Setting the Stage for a Discussion

Chapter 9
Preparing Tests, Grading, and Record Keeping 72
9.1 Preparing Tests
   9.1.a Writing Test Questions
   9.1.b Relation of Test Material to the Course
   9.1.c Determining and Maintaining Department Standards
9.2 Grading
   9.2.a General Information on Grading
   9.2.b Answer-Only Method vs. Partial-Credit Method
9.3 Record Keeping

PART • THREE
HEARING AND PRONOUNCING AMERICAN ENGLISH

Chapter 10
Getting Started 81
• **Pronunciation**
10.1 Analysis
• **Tips for Improving Pronunciation and Listening Ability**
10.2 Actively Attend to Pronunciation
10.3 Adapt to the American Way of Speaking
10.4 Know Yourself
10.5 Learn Ways to Compensate for Pronunciation Problems
• **Delivery**
10.6 Tips for Improving Delivery

Chapter 11
English Vowels and Consonants 86
11.1 Noticing Lip Shapes
11.2 Pronunciation Modeling
11.3 Comparison of English to Native-Language Vowels
11.4 Special Features of English Vowels
11.5 Comparison of English to Native-Language Consonants
11.6 Special Features of English Consonants
11.7 Consonant Combinations, Section 1
11.8 Consonant Combinations, Section 2
11.9 Comparing the Pronunciation of Words in English and the Native Language

Chapter 12
Stress Patterns in English Words and Sentences 96
12.1 English Syllables and Stress
12.2 Identifying Strong and Weak Stresses
12.3 Noun and Verb Pairs With Different Stress
12.4 Strongly Stressed Vowels, Section 1
12.5 Strongly Stressed Vowels, Section 2
12.6 Stress Patterns in Academic Words
12.7 Matching Words to Stress Patterns
12.8 More Practice in Pronouncing Longer Words
12.9 Stress in Context, Section 1
12.10 Stress in Context, Section 2
12.11 Contrastive/Emphatic Stress

Chapter 13
The Units of Fluent Speech 106
13.1 Thought Groups
13.2 Bridging

Chapter 14
Intonation and Voice Quality 109
14.1 Intonation, Section 1
14.2 Intonation, Section 2
14.3 Voice Quality

PART • FOUR

PRACTICE FOR TEACHING

Chapter 15
Learning to Give Short Explanations 117
15.1 First Five-Minute Explanation
15.2 Defining a Term
15.3 Expanding on Definitions Given in the Text
15.4 Using Descriptions to Explain
15.5 Explanations That Give Reasons
15.6 Using Conditional and Hypothetical Examples
15.7 A Longer Explanation of a Term
15.8 Evaluation of Explanations
15.9 Making a Transcript of an Audio Recording

Chapter 16
Giving Mini-Lectures to Practice Particular Teaching Acts 128
16.1 Introducing Yourself to a Class
16.2 Making Long-Term Assignments
16.3 Making Short-Term Assignments
16.4 Announcing a Test
16.5 Giving an Overview of a Unit
16.6 Returning Tests
16.7 Returning Homework
16.8 Supplementing Previous Explanations
    16.8.a Corrections
    16.8.b Additions

Chapter 17
Learning to Give Longer Presentations 133
17.1 Analyzing a Topic
17.2 Worksheet for Analysis of Textbook Chapter
17.3 Describing a Process
17.4 Connecting One Lecture to Another
17.5 Combining Definitions and Reason Giving
17.6 Explaining a Cause-Effect Relationship

Chapter 18
50-Minute Classes 139
18.1 Planning a 50-Minute Class
18.2 Giving a 50-Minute Class
18.3 Evaluation of a Faculty Member's Class

Chapter 19
Leading Discussions 142
19.1 Phrases to Use in Guiding a Discussion
19.2 Leading a Discussion of a Case Study
19.3 Worksheet for Analyzing a Case Study
19.4 Leading a Discussion of an Explanation
19.5 Evaluation Sheet for Discussions

Chapter 20
Explaining by Doing 149
20.1 An Example From the Teaching of Mathematics
20.2 Using Formulas in Other Fields

PART • FIVE

OBSERVATION

Chapter 21
Observation of Classroom Space 153
21.1 Observation of Classroom Space Used for a Graduate Course
21.2 Observation of the Classroom Space Used for an Undergraduate Course

Chapter 22
Observation of Teaching Behaviors 156
22.1 Observation of the Instructor
22.2 Observation of the Instructor's Language Acts
22.3 Observation of the Instructor's Nonverbal Acts
22.4 Observation of the Use of Organizing Language
22.5 Observation of the Use of Purpose Statements
22.6 Observation of the Use of Audience-Inclusive Language

Chapter 23
Observation of Student Behaviors 169
23.1 General Observation of Students
23.2 Observation of One Particular Student
23.3 Observation and Comparison of Three Types of Students

Chapter 24
Observation of Use of Questions by Teachers and Students 178
24.1 Observation of Student Questions
24.2 Observation of Question Interactions
24.3 Observation of Teacher Questions
24.4 Observation of Types and Purposes of Questions
24.5 Observation of the Use of Clarifying Questions
24.6 Signals That Indicate Question Types Used by Students

Chapter 25
Overall Observation of Classes 186
25.1 Observing a Class for the First Time
25.2 Observation of a Class in a Different Department

Appendix 195

ACKNOWLEDGMENTS

Training for foreign teaching assistants (FTAs) overlaps many different departments and programs of a university, and thus strong support from the highest levels of an institution is necessary for success. We would, therefore, like first to thank the many administrators whose support has made possible the development of training programs for FTAs at our various institutions: At the University of Wyoming, Dr. Joan Wadlow, former Dean of the College of Arts and Sciences; Dr. Walter Eggers, current Dean of Arts and Sciences; Dr. Thomas Dunn, Dean of the Graduate School; and Dr. Roland Barden, Associate Vice President for Academic Affairs. At Georgia State University, we would like to thank Dr. Michael Mescon, Dean of the College of Business Administration; Dr. Naomi Lynn, Dean of the College of Public and Urban Affairs; and Dr. Arthur Schreiber, Associate Dean of the College of Business Administration. Finally, at the University of Hawaii, we would like to express our gratitude to Dr. Thomas Gething, Assistant Vice President for Academic Affairs. The programs at these three institutions have been the "labs" in which the materials in this book were developed and tested.

At the same time, this book owes much to the many teachers who have discussed with us the various linguistic, cultural, and pedagogical issues involved in the development of training programs for FTAs. Among our professional colleagues, we extend particular thanks to Phil Johncock, University of Nevada-Reno, who with his fellow teachers of FTAs provided insightful evaluation and suggested additions in one of the first field tests of the materials; Phyllis Kuehn, Georgia State University, who developed GSU's system for testing the communicative competence of potential graduate teaching assistants; Phyllis Hurt, Georgia State University, who used the materials to prepare Ph.D. students to be graduate teaching assistants in the College of Business Administration; Chris Jensen, University of Wyoming, who gave unstintingly of her time and her wisdom concerning cross-cultural classrooms; and Dominique Buckley, Graham Crookes, and Gail Wnek, University of Hawaii, who field-tested parts of the final manuscript in an FTA pilot program.

Most importantly, since the book is the result of our work with non-native speakers of English who were preparing to teach U.S. undergraduates, our greatest thanks are reserved for those graduate students who have used the materials. The vast majority of them were excellent scholars who worked cooperatively and productively with us to improve their ability to teach in English to American undergraduates. As scholar-teachers, they are making important contributions to our institutions both through their research and through their teaching. We feel honored to have worked with them and to have had their advice in developing *The Foreign Teaching Assistant's Manual*.

P.B., J.C.C., M.C.P.

INTRODUCTION TO THE INSTRUCTOR

Background. Across the United States, universities are facing difficulties—sometimes of crisis proportions—caused by the increasing percentage of foreign students in graduate programs. These foreign students are a major resource for the teaching of undergraduate courses in many universities, especially in science, engineering, business, mathematics, and computer science. In these contexts, if foreign students were not available as graduate teaching assistants, the basic courses in chemistry, mathematics, and others—which are often taught through a combination of large lecture sections and smaller class discussion sections or labs—could not be adequately covered. Many of these foreign teaching assistants (FTAs) are superior researchers capable of making significant contributions in their fields. At the same time, while they usually have excellent reading and academic skills, they may have some deficiencies in speaking skills. In addition, many of them have a limited understanding of the nature of U.S. higher education in general and of U.S. undergraduates in particular. Whereas the graduate students admittedly do not always have the skills they need to be clear communicators and effective teachers, U.S. undergraduates are not always culturally sensitive or patient with outsiders. The typical U.S. undergraduate may have neither the experience nor the inclination to be understanding with the FTA who lacks the skills and experience required for effective teaching. An explosive situation is created when these graduate students are placed in front of American undergraduates.

Many universities have experienced high levels of student complaints about FTAs. A number of states have passed or soon will initiate laws that mandate testing of English for anyone allowed to teach at state colleges or universities. In response to student complaints and legislative actions, colleges and universities across the country have been establishing training programs for current or prospective FTAs. These programs range from short-term, noncredit intensive workshops prior to the beginning of the school year to term-long courses for credit. Whatever their length or credit, these courses generally include the same three areas: *cross-cultural orientation, improvement of speaking,* and *instruction in classroom teaching skills.* Many of these programs also require participants to observe classes like the ones they will be teaching to see how effective teachers conduct the classes and also to understand better how effective teachers interact with American students.

Audience. These materials are aimed at foreign graduate students who are either already teaching or who are prospective graduate teaching assistants. They are designed particularly for students whose first language is not English and who are not already experienced teachers in U.S. postsecondary education. The materials will be of value also to those who have not previously been exposed to the culture and the students of an American college/university or who would like to improve their ability to teach in such an environment. They may also be useful to the prospective FTAs by enhancing their abilities as students in the U.S. educational system.

This book presupposes an advanced level of English. As a consequence, FTAs who have serious problems in English, particularly in speaking and listening, may need to supplement this course with intensive English language instruction. In some cases, it may be advisable for new teaching assistants to take an English pronunciation or oral skills class prior to being exposed to the materials of the present text. It is strongly recommended, therefore, that each prospective or current FTA be tested in English language skills before enrolling in a course in which these materials are used and that course placement be made on the basis of test results.

Description of the Text. The text is divided into five major parts, 25 chapters. In Parts One and Two, participants carry out activities that will help them learn more about the academic culture in which they will be working and teaching. By thinking about the differences between their own educational background and that of their U.S. students, they can learn to understand better how to communicate with these students. Part Three comprises information about English pronunciation and listening. It includes a variety of activities to improve spoken delivery, pronunciation, and listening skills. Part Four initiates a program of training in classroom teaching through which the FTAs gain skill at presentation of academic content to U.S. undergraduates. This part begins with very short explanations, expands these to 15-minute presentations, and concludes with assignments for 50-minute lectures. Part Five provides materials for structured observation of effective teachers teaching American undergraduates. The observation exercises guide the FTAs to see more clearly the behaviors of teachers and of students in the university classroom. The Appendix lists cross-references to guide selection of materials from the appropriate parts of the text. For example, the place of discussion in U.S. undergraduate classes is presented in Part One; the characteristics of a discussion session are explained in Part Two; practice for discussion leaders is provided in Part Four; and observation of discussions can be arranged through use of the materials in Part Five.

General Introduction to the Materials. The text is intended to be used as a handbook in a training course for FTAs to help them prepare for teaching in an American classroom. Although individuals might benefit by working through some of the material on their own, much of the text requires a classroom setting for making videotapes and a teacher experienced in working with foreign graduate students and knowledgeable of the educational systems from which they come. The instructor should be a specialist in English as a Second Language (ESL) who is knowledgeable about the teaching process and who has a proven record of success working with an international population whose English skills are relatively advanced and who are well educated and highly motivated. The instructor also needs to know about undergraduate classrooms and students in the institution in which the FTAs will teach. Those classrooms and students are likely to be significantly different from the students and classes usually found in ESL programs. For example, while the field of ESL values small student-centered classes in which the teacher facilitates communication, most undergraduate courses in academic departments have much larger sections (35 students and up) built around the teacher as lecturer and giver of information.

A team teaching approach to the FTA course may be advisable if the ESL specialist is not very knowledgeable about the university's departments and its student population. A knowledge of the demographics of the undergraduates in the particular institution is essential. For example, not only are the entrance requirements different at different institutions, thus affecting the type of students with which the FTA will work, but different disciplines have different reputations on different campuses. Undergraduates entering required courses in departments with a reputation of being difficult for undergraduate students will already have attitudes made up of hostility and fear that can make the FTA's job especially difficult. FTAs who know about their students and their department should be able to deal with their teaching situation better than those who think all of the hostility and fear is somehow a result of their own personalities and their own teaching.

The text provides several different types of material that form the basis for classroom participation and practice. It is possible to use the entire text in a semester-length course. However, the text was not necessarily designed for this purpose. Rather, it can be viewed as a resource book from which materials can be selected according to the needs of the FTAs and the instructional purposes emphasized in the course. The design of the book also allows for selectivity in using only certain sections. Hence, it can easily be adapted to a course of less than one semester in length or to a group that has special needs or interests. The materials can, therefore, be used in short-term orientation programs as well as in term-long credit courses. Moreover, virtually all of the material can be used more than once with the same group, for example, at different times in a course. In addition to the forms provided to guide observations in Part Five, charts are given for analysis of presentations and materials in Sections 15.8, 17.2, 19.3, and 19.5. We strongly urge that you have the FTAs make adequate copies of these forms for use during the training course rather than using the original because these forms could be of use to them during their later teaching activities.

Materials are provided to fit the major categories usually included in FTA training programs: (1) orientation to U.S. academic culture and the culture of the particular institution and department; (2) training in public speaking skills and lecture organization; and (3) practice to improve the pronunciation of individual sounds as well as the more global aspects of stress, intonation, fluency, and overall comprehensibility.

The material provides a jumping-off point for many kinds of participation and practice, including discussion, observation, practice teaching, role-playing activity, group work, oral training, audiotaping, and videotaping. The material is therefore highly participatory. In order for the program to succeed, it is absolutely essential to have the cooperation and trust of all participants.

As a way to get to know participants quickly and also to determine their particular needs, the teacher may wish to have them complete right away the first activity in Part Three, where individuals are asked to make a tape in which they describe relevant points about their background and language problems for the instructor to analyze. If the instructor records the analysis as a personal message to each student, this activity will also help to establish trust and cooperation from the very beginning. To break down potential barriers such as embarrassment or shyness, it is also essential to have individuals give a brief teaching demonstration in front of the class two or three times in the first week, receiving feedback each time from the teacher and the other participants. In this way, participants get over any potentially negative feelings very early in the course, while learning what is expected of them in the way of cooperation and interaction with other members of the class. That is, rather than building up fear over a week or two while waiting to do the first presentation, the students start right away in building the experience that makes it possible for teachers to deal with their stage fright.

If possible, all demonstrations, role-playing activities, and practice teaching should be videotaped, and these videotapes used for in-depth analysis and discussion. The videotapes should be seen as opportunities not only for the person videotaped to view his/her own performance, but also for the teacher and other class members to offer feedback on that performance. The text includes many suggestions as well for participants to make audiotapes that can then be analyzed for pronunciation and other aspects of oral language. Participants should be assured that these videotapes and audiotapes are solely for the purpose of helping individuals in the class to improve their performance and will be erased by the end of the term (unless some other arrangement is explicitly made to keep the tapes on file—for example, for research purposes—and formal permission is given by the participants).

The taping activities are integral to the course envisioned by the authors of these materials, as are the large number of observational assignments. The observational assignments, like the video and audio assignments, are intended to provide useful information to participants. But they are further intended to help participants develop their observational and analytical skills so that they can continue to improve as teachers after the course has finished.

INTRODUCTION TO THE TEACHING ASSISTANT

This text is based on several years of experience by the authors in training foreign teaching assistants (FTAs) to be more effective in carrying out their teaching responsibilities. Many U.S. undergraduates complain that they cannot understand the pronunciation of their FTAs. It is true that some FTAs have such great difficulties with spoken English that they are very difficult to understand. Many other FTAs have few problems with American English in one-to-one communication (e.g., conversations with friends) but have not yet learned how to use the special features of spoken English in the classroom (louder voice, longer turns, being in control of communication, etc.).

In many cases, however, the miscommunication is based on two areas other than mispronunciation or lack of skill at using the English of the classroom. Both of these areas can be considered the results of cross-cultural differences:
1. FTAs and U.S. undergraduates frequently have quite different ideas about the purposes and methods of higher education.
2. FTAs and U.S. undergraduates frequently have quite different ideas about the proper relationships between teacher and student both in class and outside the classroom.

In addition, many FTAs (like many of their U.S. peers) often have no experience preparing lessons and presenting information in front of a class of students; that is, they lack a background in teaching in U.S. classrooms.

This textbook is designed for the FTA who is already fluent and understandable in spoken English. Students with severely dysfunctional speaking (e.g., those who speak with a very strong accent or who have trouble responding spontaneously or expressing their ideas in English) should participate in a training course in advanced pronunciation and speaking prior to taking this training course. Those with major problems in listening to fluent American English may also not be ready to teach American students and so may be advised to supplement this course with an advanced listening course or with independent work in a language laboratory. The text has five major parts, which are designed for use in a coordinated program of FTA training. You will work from all five parts at the same time rather than working through the text from start to finish. Part One: "Preparatory Activities" has activities through which you will learn about differences between your educational background and that of your U.S. students. Understanding of these differences will be useful to you as you teach because you can better meet your students' needs and better anticipate their attitudes and actions. Part Two: "Background to Teaching" focuses on the skills needed for effective teaching in this culture, including descriptions of the various types of speaking done by a teacher. In Part Three: "Hearing and Pronouncing American English," explanations and exercises are offered to help improve your skills in both speaking and listening. These activities have been found effective for helping high-intermediate and advanced speakers to communicate more clearly in spoken English. Part Four: "Practice for Teaching" provides activities to improve your ability to be an effective presenter of information in the classroom context. These activities range from the giving of 5-minute explanations to the presentation of a complete 50-minute class. Part Five: "Observation" sends you out to learn more about teaching in the U.S. by carefully focused observation of the various activities that take place in an undergraduate classroom.

Thus, your training program will involve the following:
- Gaining understanding of the purposes, methods, and realities of U.S. education
- Learning more about cultural differences that can hamper communication
- Improving your ability to speak and understand English
- Building skills in classroom communication
- Observing U.S. teachers and undergraduates as they interact in the classroom

Through the wide variety of practical activities presented in the text, you can gain the skills, knowledge, and confidence necessary for success in fulfilling your teaching responsibilities.

PART·ONE
PREPARATORY ACTIVITIES

Chapter ♦ 1

Background to U.S. Education

♦ OVERVIEW

The educational system of a country is a reflection of the culture of that country and is often also the principal medium for maintaining that culture. Thus it becomes important for anyone who will be part of an educational system to understand how it is organized and how it reflects the philosophy, beliefs, and ideals of a culture. This section will help you explore how the educational system of the United States is organized and how its philosophy of education reflects American cultural values. It will also help you to understand the organization of the university in which you are now to become part of the group of people who teach. At the same time that you are engaged in the background and discussion activities in this chapter, you should be carrying out some of the observation activities in Part Five to see how the ideas presented in this section are evidenced in classroom settings.

Knowing how education is viewed in this country and how your students expect you as a teaching assistant to act will help you to become a more effective teaching assistant.

◆ ELEMENTARY AND HIGH SCHOOL EDUCATION

1.1 Background Assignment

For each of the following questions, provide the information asked for as it applies to the majority of situations in your country. If there are notable exceptions, indicate them.

1. Do most children go to nursery school or preschool? At what age do they begin? What is the purpose of their being in nursery school or preschool? What are they expected to learn? Do parents pay for their children to attend school? If so, how much?

2. Do most children go to kindergarten? At what age do they begin? What is the purpose of their being in kindergarten? What are they expected to learn? Do parents pay for their children to attend school? If so, how much?

3. At what age do children begin elementary school? What percentage of children attend? Who chooses which school they will attend? Do parents pay for their children to attend elementary school? How much?

4. When children finish elementary school (approximately six years), how is it determined who will continue in school? Are different children sent to different types of middle schools (junior high schools, approximately three years)? On what basis is that choice or assignment made? Do parents pay for their children to attend the middle school? How much?

5. Who goes to high school (or the equivalent, approximately three to four years)? On what basis are they admitted? Who chooses which school each student will attend? Do the students have any choice of the classes they take? If not, who decides which classes they must take? Do parents pay for their children to attend high school? How much?

6. What is the purpose of elementary and high school education in your country? How does that affect how students are taught? How does it affect how students react to going to school?

1.2 Discussion Assignment

Using the answers to the questions in 1.1, consider the following ideas. You will need to have someone in your group who can thoroughly and accurately describe elementary and high school education in the United States, especially that of the students in the university you are now attending.

Share with the others in your group the most important information about elementary and high school education in your country. If possible, explore how that education reflects the cultural values of your country. Then fill in the chart below.

	In your country	In the U.S.
Nursery or Preschool		
Kindergarten		
Elementary School		
Middle School		
High School		

What are the major differences between the elementary and high school systems in other countries and the system in the U.S.?

◆ ORGANIZATION OF HIGHER EDUCATION

1.3 Background Assignment

For each of the following questions, provide the information asked for as it applies to the majority of situations in your country. If there are notable exceptions, indicate them.

1. Who goes to high school (or the equivalent)? How are they selected, if they are? How is their choice of study determined? What educational alternatives are there besides high school?

2. Who becomes a university or college student? Is there a difference between a college and a university?

3. How are students chosen for college/university admission? What percentage of students who apply for admission are accepted?

4. What does it cost for a student to attend a college/university? Who pays?

5. How are colleges/universities funded?

6. How are colleges/universities administered? Who chooses the administrators?

7. Who sets the curricula? Are there any agencies outside the institution that evaluate or endorse the various curricula?

1.4 Discussion Assignment

Using the answers to the questions in 1.3, consider the following comparisons. You will need to have someone in your group who can thoroughly and accurately describe the university you are now attending.

Share with the others in your group the most important information about the ways universities and colleges operate in your country. Then fill in the chart below.

	Universities in your country	The university you are now attending
Administration		
Funding		
Responsibility for curricula		
Cost and source of funds (for students)		
Selection of students		

What do you think are the most important differences? Why?

Chapter 1 Background to U.S. Education

◆ ANALYSIS OF FACULTY ROLES AND BEHAVIORS

1.5 Background Assignment

For each of the following questions, provide the information asked for as it applies to the majority of situations in your country. If there are notable exceptions, indicate them.

1. How does a person prepare to teach in preschool or elementary school? Are these teachers primarily male or female?

2. How does a person prepare to teach in high school? Are these teachers primarily male or female? Are there certain subjects that are taught more often by males than females and vice versa? Give examples.

3. How does a person prepare to become a college or university professor? Are professors primarily male or female, or does that vary according to the field the professors teach in? Give examples.

4. How are elementary school teachers expected to treat their students?

5. How are high school teachers expected to treat their students?

6. How are college or university professors expected to treat their students?

7. What methods do university professors most often use in their classes (e.g., lectures, discussions, questioning students, etc.)?

8. According to the students in your country, what are the characteristics of a good professor?

9. How do students treat high school teachers? How do they treat professors?

10. What is the social status of elementary school teachers? of high school teachers? of college or university professors?

11. How is a degree from a university or college viewed by society at large in your country?

12. What is the goal of education?

13. What is the proper effect that education should have on the individual?

1.6 Discussion Assignment

You will need to have someone in your group who can answer the questions in 1.5 as they apply to the university you are now attending. Using your answers as well, fill in the following chart. (You might also want to use information you collected from Part Five.)

	Other countries' colleges/universities	The university you are now attending
Status of professors		
Duties of professors		
Place of teaching assistants		
Characteristics of a good professor		
Goal of education		
Desired effect of education on individuals		

◆ ANALYSIS OF STUDENT ROLES AND BEHAVIORS

1.7 Background Assignment

For each of the following questions, provide the information asked for as it applies to the majority of situations in your country. If there are notable exceptions, indicate them.

1. How is a student's field of study at a college/university determined?

2. In college/university-level classes, how are the students tested? How often? Who determines the grades and how? (For example, are there outside readers for the exams? Is there a set of standard grading criteria that are applied to all exams? Does the standard vary with the collective performance of the students, so that the best performance receives the top grade and other grades are figured based on that; or is the standard rigid, no matter what the performance of the students may be?)

3. What is the importance and purpose of books? How do students use books? What kinds of books are used (textbooks, etc.)?

4. How do high school and college/university students study? (For example, do they memorize, copy material from books, integrate theory and examples, do extra reading on their own, prepare only for exams without having to hand in practice examples or homework?)

5. What kinds of tests do students take in a college/university? How often are tests given?

6. In what ways is it accepted for students to work together or study together on an assignment?

7. If a university student does not understand what is going on in class, what should he/she do?

8. If a student does not like the way a professor teaches, who will the student talk to about that, if anyone (e.g., other students, parents, the university administration, etc.)?

9. Are students asked to evaluate the performance of professors? If so, how?

1.8 Discussion Assignment

Using your answers from 1.7, contrast college-/university-level students in your country with those in the university you are now attending. You will need to have someone in your group who can answer the questions in 1.7 as they apply to the undergraduates at the institution you are now attending. (You might also want to include information from Part Five.) Someone from your group will be designated to lead the discussion.

You should consider the following questions:

1. To what extent do students expect teachers/professors to give them very specific assignments?

2. To what extent do students expect to be able to determine on their own what is important to learn from a given assignment, a particular lecture, and so on? To what extent do teachers/professors expect students to identify important ideas, major concepts, and so on?

3. How and when can students indicate to professors that they do not understand something?

4. If a student is not satisfied with his/her grade on a test or assignment, what can he/she do about it?

5. What are the best ways to study?

6. How should students act in a classroom?

Chapter ♦ 2

Departmental Relations

♦ OVERVIEW

American universities are divided into colleges (or schools or divisions) that are further divided into departments. These departments have certain organizational patterns that affect the way you will be expected to work as a teaching assistant (TA). Understanding how the department works and makes decisions about such matters as setting course requirements, awarding teaching assistantships, and evaluating performance can be useful to you in preparing to become a part of that department, both as a student and as a teaching assistant.

Although departments may appear to be organized in similar ways (i.e., each may have a chairperson or head), they often work in different ways to accomplish the same tasks (i.e., the chairperson may or may not be the one to make the assignments of duties for teaching assistants). This chapter is designed to help you analyze the department in which you will be an assistant so that you will be better prepared to meet the expectations of that department in your performance of the teaching duties assigned to you.

◆ ORGANIZATION OF DEPARTMENTS

2.1 Background Assignment

For each of the following questions, you will need to consult with people in the academic department in which you are going to be a graduate student and in which you will be a teaching assistant.

1. In which college (school, division) in your university is the department located? How many departments are there in that college/school/division?
2. What is the name and title of the person who is the chief administrator in the department? How long has that person been in that position?
3. How many full-time tenure-track faculty are in the department?
   How many full professors?
   How many associate professors?
   How many assistant professors?
   How many at other ranks (indicate the rank)?
4. How many part-time and/or non-tenure-track faculty are there?
5. Are there subsections in the department (i.e., a group of faculty who all have the same or similar fields in which they work)? Do these subsections have designated leaders or administrators to whom other faculty report or with whom they are expected or required to consult in making decisions about curriculum, admitting graduate students, and so on?
6. Who in the department makes the decision about which graduate students to admit?
7. Who determines which graduate students are awarded assistantships?
8. Are there differences in the assignments given faculty of different ranks? (For example, do full professors teach fewer classes than assistant professors?)
9. How many support staff are there in the department?
   Administrative assistants
   Secretaries
   Technicians
   Clerks
   Others (indicate their positions)
10. With which of the staff will you be expected or will you need to interact? What sort of interaction is needed in each case?

	Name	Position	Interaction
a.			
b.			
c.			
d.			
e.			

2.2 Directory of Your Department

Make a chart to collect names, office numbers, phone numbers, titles, and academic specialties for key people in your department. To have copies for further use, make at least three copies of the chart before you fill it in.

Discuss with other participants the ways that you got this information and any additional things that you learned about your department or the university while you were filling in the form.

	Name	Office	Phone	Title	Academic specialty

1. Chair/Head: _____

2. Assistant chair/Head: _____

3. TA adviser: _____

4. Graduate student adviser: _____

5. My adviser: _____

6. Additional information: _____

_____
_____
_____
_____
_____
_____
_____
_____
_____
_____
_____
_____
_____
_____
_____
_____

◆ ROLE OF GRADUATE TEACHING ASSISTANTS

2.3 Background Assignment

The assignments that graduate teaching assistants are given vary among the departments within a university. In answering the questions below, you will need to consult with people who are familiar with the situation in your department (experienced graduate teaching assistants, the graduate adviser, perhaps the department secretary). As you approach these people, be sure to indicate that you are seeking information, *not* questioning or challenging the system.

1. Are there different types of teaching duties given to different graduate TAs in your department? (For example, do some lecture to students while others lead discussion or problem sessions and still others conduct labs?) List the various types of duties.

    a. _____

    b. _____

    c. _____

    d. _____

2. Is the TA assigned to work with a particular faculty member (who then decides what the TA will do) or to a particular course (with the expected duties the same no matter who is teaching the course)? Perhaps both arrangements exist. Describe the situation in your department.

3. Are TAs responsible for awarding a grade to their students? On what basis is that grade to be figured? What percentage of the total course grade does it represent?

4. If TAs lead discussion or problem sessions, are they expected to read the text and attend the lectures that the undergraduates do? If not, how are TAs to know what material the undergraduates are supposed to know?

5. In the discussion or problem session, is the TA expected to prepare questions or examples, or is he/she supposed to respond to student questions? How will the TA know which to do? Does the professor in charge indicate to the TA the important ideas/concepts to be covered? If not, how does the TA decide what is important?

6. If the TAs are assigned as lab assistants, what are they expected to do? (This sounds like a simple question, but it may be quite complicated. Get as much detail as you can about what is expected in each type of lab setting.)

    a. in an introductory-level course:

    b. in an intermediate course:

16 Chapter 2 *Departmental Relations*

   c. in an advanced course:

7. To whom do the TAs report? Is there one person in charge of several TAs? Or does each TA report to his/her own major professor/course coordinator or supervisor?

8. Who evaluates the performance of the TA and how?
   a. students:

   b. a TA coordinator:

   c. the major professor/course coordinator or supervisor:

   d. others:

9. Are TAs expected to hold office hours? If so, how many a week? Where? What if students can't come during those hours?

10. How many of the TAs in your department are foreign students? What percentage of all TAs does this represent?

2.4 Discussion Assignment

Using your answers from 2.3, share with others in your group the responsibilities of teaching assistants in your department. How are they alike or different from those of others in your group?

List the specific types of activities required of TAs and then consider the type of skill needed to carry out each one. The responsibility for leading a problem session has been done as an illustration.

Assigned Task

a. Lead problem session

Skills Needed

1. Understand students' questions
2. Know what material students are expected to know
3. Be able to explain problems
4. Be able to recognize why student is having difficulty with problem

b. _____

c. _____

d. _____

e. _____

Chapter • 3
Profiles of American Students

♦ OVERVIEW

In each educational system, students and teachers interact in ways that are predetermined by the customs of that culture. Appropriate behavior for students in one culture may, therefore, be seen as unusual, rude, or shocking behavior in another. For example, are students expected to ask questions of the teacher if they do not understand the material being presented, or are they supposed to find the answers to questions on their own, outside of class? A student who asks questions in a culture in which students are expected to find their own answers will probably not be considered a good student, in fact may be seen as a poor student. Or, for another example, should students speak to teachers first (or at all) or wait to be spoken to? Can students disagree with the teacher in class (or in private) or challenge what the teacher has said? The answers will vary according to the student's culture.

This chapter is designed to help you understand the appropriate and accepted roles for students in American culture and specifically those you will encounter in the particular teaching assignment you will have in the institution you are now attending. Certain underlying assumptions about the appropriate roles for students in American culture are discussed in this chapter. (The appropriate roles for teachers are discussed in Chapter 4.) It is important for you to remember, though, that these are generalizations about students and teachers, and that there will always be exceptions. There will also be variations among and within different postsecondary institutions in this country. You need to be aware of both the general patterns and the exceptions or variations you may find among your own students in order to be a successful teaching assistant.

3.1 In the Classroom

3.1.a Preparing Before Class

Students are expected to do some preparation before they attend a class or lab session. This includes preparing before a problem session or review session as well. In reality, however, the amount of preparation students do depends on a variety of factors, including the expectations of the institution in general, the expectations communicated to the students by the teacher, and the individual motivation of each student.

Some institutions require that students take a great part of the responsibility for their own learning. In these cases, it is expected that students will be "self-starters" who can work independently and do not need to be told in detail each time what to do before the next class/lab session. Institutions that have this expectation are usually those with high admissions standards and very selective admissions policies. In such cases, students may attend the lecture having done all the assigned reading, as well as perhaps some outside reading. They attend a lab ready to begin the lab work because they have read the lab procedure carefully and have done all the pre-lab work completely. If there is a problem session or review session, they come prepared to ask specific questions because they have carefully reviewed the material on their own. The teacher may need to do no more than hand out a syllabus at the beginning of the term, with the reading/lab assignments indicated, and then go to the class expecting to find the students ready to benefit from the lecture, discussion, demonstration, or experiment, and prepared to answer questions or engage in discussion. Students who act in this fashion are also likely to be those who get assignments in on time without having to be reminded.

Many institutions would prefer to have their students behave as those described in the preceding paragraph. However, in reality, their students may need to be reminded of reading assignments or due dates for outside work. They may or may not prepare thoroughly and may not get assignments in on time unless they are reminded often and penalized if they do not. Such students may be prepared on some days and not on others. They may be able to discuss, based on their reading, or they may expect the teacher to tell them the important points without their having done the reading. Sometimes students adopt this type of preparation behavior because, although the institution and the teacher have said that they expect students to be prepared, the teacher has indicated in other ways that preparation is not really necessary. The teacher may do that by always going over the reading material in detail, by just repeating what is in the book, or by not insisting that assignments be handed in on time. Given these subtle signals, it will not take students long to realize that being prepared is not required.

In all institutions there are those students who do little if any preparation for class or lab. The number of these depends to some extent on the admission policies and the culture of the institution. These students expect that the teacher will indicate the important material in each lesson, without the student having to read or prepare for class. They may also expect to be told exactly what to do to complete an assignment or study for an examination. They may want to be "spoon-fed," that is, to have the teacher take the responsibility for their learning. It is not a good idea to let students operate in this fashion.

A skillful teacher will give clear signals about how much responsibility the students must take for their learning. For example, making and maintaining a policy that all assignments must be in on time will soon get the message across to any student who is concerned about being successful. Not repeating each point in the textbook will indicate that the students are expected to read the relevant sections before coming to class. It is not enough, though, just to say that work must be done on time. The teacher must follow through, must make the penalties for failure to do so clear to the students, and then must invoke those penalties when work is not completed on time. For example, a paper that is not turned in may not be accepted late, resulting in a grade of "0" (zero) for the assignment; or, the grade may be lowered if the paper is late. Such penalties should be indicated in writing and consistently applied according to the written policy.

Another factor that affects how a student prepares for a class is the student's own motivation. It has become an expectation that many young people will attend a college or university. Some of them go to college without having given much thought about why they are going; they are simply fulfilling an expectation that has been communicated to them through their parents, the television, and their peers. Having no particular motivation for attending school, they may have very little motivation for preparing for their classes. Such students often attend open admissions schools, where they can be admitted without having to do much in the way of preparation or application. Other students may prepare thoroughly for some classes but not for others. These students see courses outside their particular majors as extraneous to their goals; they do not understand the idea that a university/college education is intended to provide one with not only a concentration in a specific subject but also a broad general education. Often these students are found in introductory required courses outside their major field of study. Although they are able to do well, they may not apply themselves in some subjects. A third type of student prepares thoroughly and rigorously because he/she wants to succeed; such students are self-motivated. Their goal may be to make excellent grades, for example. Often, these students are found in schools with highly selective admissions policies, though they may be found in any college or university.

You should determine what the situation is on your campus, in your department, and for the course you are to be an assistant in. Then you should try to signal your expectations, both in written and oral form, as clearly as possible to your students. But if your expectations are different from those of others teaching the same course or lab, you may find that students are resentful.

Assignment

1. Which of these profiles of students best describes the students you teach? You may want to ask experienced TAs or faculty in your department for their opinions on this question.

2. Given the type of students in your institution, what kind of behavior can you expect from them in terms of their preparation before class?

3. Is the course in which you are to teach a required course for nonmajors? If so, which students are required to take it?

4. What do the answers to these questions tell you about your need to have and enforce strict policies?

5. Does your department (or institution) have policies about such matters as missed classes and late work? What are they? If the department or institution does not have any policies, do you need to set some for your classes? If so, what might they be?

3. 1. b Asking Questions

The American educational system encourages students to ask questions. The philosophy of education in this country includes the idea that students should be involved in an interactive learning process; that is, they should not just sit passively and accept or memorize what the teacher says. Consequently, students have been taught from their elementary school days to ask questions when they are not sure, when they do not understand, or when they would like to get some more information.

Most questions that students ask are intended to help them understand the material or concepts underlying the lesson better. Although they may not always sound like questions (see 6.8 and Chapter 24 for additional information and suggestions for observations), their purpose is to seek information or to clarify what the student thinks is the case. It is not uncommon, especially in smaller classes, for students to interrupt a lecture to ask questions. This is not considered rude, in most cases, especially if the student has signaled in an appropriate way that he/she wishes to ask a question. (In small classes or in discussion or review sessions, no signal may be needed; the student may just begin to speak.) Even if some students are too shy to speak up often, especially in a large class, they will still consider it their right to ask questions when they want to exercise that right.

Sometimes, students ask questions that challenge the truth or validity of a statement made by a teacher. The educational system in this culture is based on the idea that students should learn not just information, but how to arrive at conclusions, to solve problems, and to analyze—in short, how to think in ways accepted as logical in U.S. culture. As part of this process, students are often asked to show how they got an answer (rather than just what the answer is). American students, therefore, find it perfectly normal to think that in many cases there may be more than one right answer. Moreover, the right to have and to express individual opinions is considered basic in American culture; and from this perspective it is understandable that American students may feel that they can challenge what the teacher says. In the ideal situation, that challenge should include a justification, an explanation for why the student thinks there is a different answer from the one given by the teacher. On occasion, however, students ask questions to challenge the authority of the teacher. In postsecondary education, the teacher is often seen as a strong authority figure against whom some students wish to rebel. Sometimes the challenge appears to be (and is) only a way of attacking what the student sees as the power, status, or authority of the teacher. It also happens on occasion that students raise questions to challenge or disagree with the text materials or with another student.

In a few situations, students may use questions as a way of diverting the focus of the class. This is known as "getting the teacher off the track." Such questions do not relate to the main points of the class, although they may be of interest to some students.

Students expect to be able to ask questions, and they also expect that the teacher will accept most questions (except those that are highly disruptive or frivolous).

Assignment

Use the observation sheets in Part Five and visit some classes like the ones you will teach.

1. Did students ask any questions that challenged or disputed what the teacher said? If so, be prepared to share the exact wording of such questions with other participants in the TA training course.

2. If so, how did the teacher respond to them?

3. Were there disruptive or frivolous questions? If so, be prepared to share the exact wording of such questions with the other participants in the TA training course.

4. How did the teacher respond to them?

3. 1. c Discussing

Discussion is often used as a means of teaching. Because the emphasis in the American educational system is on the method of inquiry, on problem solving, and on ways of reaching conclusions, discussion can be a learning process for the students. Students expect to be able to discuss, in order to develop their ideas and opinions and to present them for reactions.

The objective for a discussion may be to clarify course content by encouraging students to engage actively in processing what they are learning. Or it may be to illustrate the process of learning or of solving a problem. It almost always has as one of its objectives getting students involved in the subject.

There are important differences between lecturing and leading a discussion. The lecture is designed to present a body of knowledge about a subject in a structured way that will allow students to acquire more information about the subject. (See Part Four for ideas about presenting a lecture.) The purpose of the lecture is to convey knowledge. Most if not all of the talking is done by the teacher, who may use visual aids (chalkboard, handouts, films, overhead transparencies, etc.) to clarify and reinforce what he/she says. Questions may or may not be encouraged from the students; if they are, their purpose is also to clarify what the speaker has said.

A discussion is designed for a different purpose. In a discussion, a group of people talk with one another in order to arrive at a mutually satisfactory understanding or solution to a problem. In a discussion, the emphasis may be on the process of arriving at some solution rather than on reaching a particular solution. The discussion leader, unlike the lecturer, may do very little of the talking; the leader's role is to lead the group to express different points of view, while keeping the group from straying from the purpose of the discussion and individual members from becoming too argumentative. Both disagreement and argument are acceptable means of testing the soundness of ideas, but cooperation is paramount to the group discussion process. It is the function of the discussion leader to make sure that cooperation toward reaching a solution to the problem remains the primary goal of the group. (See Chapters 8 and 19 for suggestions on leading a discussion.)

Another difference between lectures and discussions is that, while the interaction between the teacher and the students in a lecture often occurs only at selected points or at the end of the lecture in the form of questions and answers, there is constant interaction in a discussion. Such interaction between the students does not occur in a lecture. As a rule, the discussion leader may spend several minutes without talking while the students discuss among themselves.

Students will take part in discussions to varying degrees, depending on their own personalities and on what signals the teacher gives. Some students are basically shy; they do not easily take part in discussions because they do not like to draw attention to themselves. Others like being in the "spotlight" and may want to talk, whether or not they have much of substance to say.

A third difference between lectures and discussions is that the primary medium of communication is speech. Most of the time, visual aids are not used in a discussion. This means that listening skills become very important, for both the participants and the discussion leader. The participants must listen to the input from the other students; if they do not, they will not be able to proceed with the discussion, or they may find that they have lost the train of thought of the discussion. A student cannot respond to what another student has said if the first student did not hear it correctly. The teacher must have good listening skills, too, in order to know just when to intervene in the discussion or to help clarify points or resolve misunderstandings or disputes.

American students are used to taking part in discussions. Although some will be vocal and more eager to participate than others, all of them have had some previous experience with discussion. Some may not realize, however, that the purpose of a discussion is to learn how to solve a problem or demonstrate that they can support a statement with adequate evidence; they may therefore feel that discussion is either a way to "kill time" or simply a bother. In other cases, shy students may find talking in a group uncomfortable. Nevertheless, almost all understand the rules for a discussion—when it is appropriate to interrupt, how to question or challenge the ideas of others in the group, and so on. (See Chapters 6 and 24 for more on questions and challenges.)

Assignment

1. What topics in the course you will teach might be appropriate for a discussion?

    a. _____
    b. _____
    c. _____
    d. _____

2. Visit a class in which a discussion is used. Use some of the observation guides in Part Five to help you. (Also, see Chapter 8 for more information about discussions.)

3. 1. d Challenging and Disputing

Many American students will engage in behaviors in a class or lab that may appear rude at first. Rather than accepting what the teacher says, they may openly disagree with the conclusion reached, with the method used to solve a problem, or even with the answer to a problem. American students have been trained by their previous educational experiences that not only are challenging and disputing allowed but in some cases they are expected. For example, a teacher may purposely make an incorrect statement, with the expectation that students will challenge the statement and be able to support their challenge with the correct information.

Some professors conduct their classes with the expectation that students may interrupt at any point to challenge or dispute what is being presented. Such classes usually put a premium on the learning process rather than the presentation of specific information. For example, in a management class, a case study may be analyzed in a certain way by the professor, who is then challenged by a student who has a different analysis to present. Or in a mathematics class, a student may dispute the method used to solve a problem, offering another method as equally (if not more) efficient.

American students expect that they can challenge or dispute what is said in class. Ideally, they should be able to defend an alternate point of view, method of solution, or analysis. Sometimes, they are better at disagreeing than at explaining why they disagree. Then the teacher needs to be able to encourage them to explain why they challenged or disputed what was said; they should not expect to disagree without being required to explain why.

Students may challenge or dispute statements by another student or the teacher for many reasons. A challenge to a statement made by the instructor or another student may represent a bona fide misunderstanding or disagreement about facts. When such a challenge is made during class time, it may provide a valuable opportunity for the instructor to clarify a point of confusion or to discuss varying points of view on a particular issue. In other cases, challenges may represent attempts by students to show off, to take control of the class, or to question the instructor's competence. Students who are bored or frustrated about a lesson or a course may raise issues simply to "stir up" the class or to get the attention of the instructor or of other students. In extreme cases, a classroom dispute may represent a personal attack on another student or on the instructor.

Assignment

If you are not used to the idea of students challenging or disputing, you may find this behavior unsettling. (See Part Five for observations of students as one way of determining how students in your institution/department act in this role.)

Learning how to handle classroom challenges and disputes is an important part of successful teaching. Work with a group to consider the answers to the following questions.

1. What are the circumstances under which a challenge or dispute during class time is warranted, in your opinion?

2. Under what circumstances is such an occurrence not warranted?

3. Are certain ways of raising a challenge or dispute unacceptable?

4. What do you think is the appropriate way for a student to challenge or dispute a statement by another student?

by the faculty member?

5. How would you handle a challenge which you suspect might be a personal attack?

6. How would you handle challenges or disputes about the subject matter of the class?

7. What are the warning signals that a challenge or dispute may not be directed toward the topic of the class but may instead represent a personal attack on a student or the instructor?

8. How would you handle a case in which a certain student or students continually interrupt your lectures or explanations with challenges?

3. 1. e Learning Styles

Because of the nature of the American educational system, it is expected that different students may learn differently. In fact, recent research supports the idea that each individual has a preferred style of learning. Some students find that they learn best when they are allowed to experiment or find the answer by themselves. Others find it more comfortable to memorize main ideas or important points after they have been pointed out by someone else, usually the teacher. Some students like to study with music in the background; others prefer to study in absolute quiet. Some work best in the early morning; others, late at night.

In addition, there are different ways by which students can best take in information. Some students are visual learners; they need to see the material before they can understand or remember it. These learners often take copious notes or write out all the main ideas when studying for a test. Also, they may invent diagrams or charts to use when learning new material.

Others are primarily auditory learners; they learn best by hearing the ideas or information. For them, the lecture format can be very useful because the primary channel for gaining information is their ears. Such students may say the material over and over to themselves in order to understand or remember it. During class, they may be seen whispering to themselves as a way to hear the material.

Some students are tactile learners; that is, they learn better by touching objects and feeling the texture or shape of them. These students often choose majors that allow them to work with their hands.

And there are kinesthetic learners. These students engage in some sort of physical activity in order to understand or remember. For example, a kinesthetic learner may trace the outline of a particular geometric shape or connect certain body movements with specific ideas. Kinesthetic learners may also increase retention by the physical act of note-taking.

Most learners combine the characteristics described above. For example, for some people it is helpful to write down the material to be learned. This is a combination of kinesthetic and visual learning: writing is a kinesthetic activity, and viewing what has been or is being written is a visual activity. Others may combine visual and auditory techniques, by reading aloud or by writing notes and whispering to themselves.

Any of the learning styles described is allowed for students, so long as their activity in class or during an exam does not disturb other students. For example, it would not be considered acceptable for an auditory learner to talk out loud during an exam. Nor could a kinesthetic learner get up during a class and move about the room freely. However, in keeping with the underlying philosophy of American education that each student should learn according to his or her capability, there is the accompanying idea that each student should learn in the way most effective for him or her. This means that good teachers need to use a variety of ways of passing on information to students and of encouraging them in their efforts at learning and problem solving. (See Part Two for suggestions on presenting material in class in a variety of ways and Chapter 7 for how to use visual aids.)

It is important to remember that, whichever style of learning a student may find most comfortable, the goal of the learning will be the same. In American classrooms that goal is for the student to understand how to reach conclusions, solve problems, explain a theory—and *not just to be able to memorize the material*.

Assignment

After you have filled out the following sheet, discuss your answers with other participants in the course. Be sure to compare your answers with those of someone who is thoroughly familiar with the expected teaching and learning behaviors at the institution where you will be teaching.

1. Characterize your own approach to learning. Do you believe that there is a particular learning style or classroom approach which is most successful for students? Can you characterize it?

26 Chapter 3 *Profiles of American Students*

2. Characterize the learning styles of successful and unsuccessful students in your culture by listing the learning behaviors that they each engage in.

Successful Learning Style	Unsuccessful Learning Style

3. What are the behaviors needed for a student to be successful in learning the subject you are going to teach? You will need to know the expectations of the course you will teach, that is, the type and number of assignments. Why are these behaviors necessary? One necessary behavior has been analyzed as an illustration.

Behavior	Reason
a. Ability to read quickly with high retention rate	In political science, there is a great deal of material to read, and details such as dates and places are important.
b. _____	_____
c. _____	_____
d. _____	_____
e. _____	_____

4. What can a student do to improve his/her learning approach?

5. What can a teacher do to help students who are not very successful learners?

28 Chapter 3 *Profiles of American Students*

3. 2 Outside the Classroom

3. 2. a Asking for Help

Although students may ask for help or indicate that they do not understand during a class, they sometimes wait until after the class/lab is finished to do this. Depending on the culture of the institution that you are now attending, they may or may not be encouraged to ask questions before, during, or after class.

In some institutions, it is expected that teachers will be in their offices not only during office hours but at other times as well. Then students may feel free to drop by at any time to ask for help. At the other extreme is the institution in which most faculty are on campus only for classes; students may be required to make appointments to seek help.

Whatever the situation, most students will feel that they have the right to ask for help. This is in contrast to students in other cultures, who may feel that it is their responsibility alone to find out whatever it is they do not understand. American students see it as part of the job of the teacher to help them; it is part of the teacher's responsibility to provide assistance, not a favor that the teacher does for students.

Analyzing student course evaluation forms is one way to determine how important the students and others at your institution consider your being available for help. If there is a question or statement similar to "is available to help students when needed," you can be sure that at that institution the teacher's role as helper is considered important and that students will view negatively the teacher who is too busy or not available when they want help.

Of course, you cannot spend all of your time waiting for students to approach you. It is important to do two things, however: signal clearly to students that you *are* willing to help, and also signal *when* you are available. For example, you might say on the first day of class: "My office hours are from 10:00 to 11:00 A.M., Mondays, Wednesdays, and Fridays. I realize some of you may have classes then; but if you will see me just before or after this class, I'll be glad to find a time that is mutually convenient for us to meet." This signals that you are willing to help but that arrangements may need to be made in advance if a student wants to find you in your office.

3. 2. b Questioning Grades

American students are often very conscious of and concerned about their grades. By the time they reach a college or university, they have been shown in a variety of ways that grades are important, not just as indicators of their progress, but also in some cases as the determining factor in their eligibility for certain activities, such as sports and social organizations, as well as admission to certain universities, eligibility for financial aid and scholarships, and other awards. Grades are also of the utmost importance to students planning to go on to graduate or professional schools, as the grade-point average is an important factor in competitive admissions. Consequently, students want to know exactly what their grades are and how those grades are arrived at. They also feel that they have the right to ask the teacher about grades that they do not understand or do not agree with.

Some students will question the grade on homework or on quizzes or tests because they are not sure how the grade was calculated. One way of helping to avoid such questions is to make your grading policy very clear. (See Chapter 9 for suggestions.) If a student continues to question a grade even after you have explained the grading policy, you can refer the student to that policy and repeat or paraphrase its content.

Other times, a student questions grades in the hope of getting the teacher to change the grade to a better one. Because some teachers might have changed their grades in the past, students think (or at least hope) that they can convince another teacher or teaching assistant to do that, too. These students may appear very aggressive and argumentative. Again, the best way to handle this is to have a clearly articulated grading policy and then to refer the student to it.

In some cases, the student may threaten to go to your supervisor or department chair to have the grade changed. Some students will not accept a teaching assistant's evaluation as the final one. Usually, your supervisor will support you, if you have done a conscientious and fair job of grading the work in the first place. If a student should tell you that he/she is going to your supervisor, you should contact the supervisor and explain that the student is coming, what the dispute is about, and how you arrived at the grade.

If the grading policy was not set by you, tell the student that and try to explain what the policy is and, if possible, why it was set that way. If it is beyond your control to change a grade, tell the student that, too, and explain what, if anything, the student can do to have the grade reevaluated.

If you feel that there may be some justification for the student's request for a change in grade, you may consult with your supervisor or chair to help reevaluate the student's work. In the case in which a student is justified in expecting a grade change—for example, if some error in calculation or evaluation of the student's work has been made—the official grade change policy of your institution should be consulted and proper documentation made.

Usually, students will be satisfied with an explanation about the grade that indicates that there was a clearly formulated grading policy in place, that you used it consistently, and that you were fair in the grading. American students are very concerned about the issue of fairness and very sensitive to the idea that one student may have been given some kind of advantage that others were not. If you can show them that all were treated fairly, they will be more easily satisfied.

Assignment

See 9.2 for suggestions about grading and 6.8 for information about asking and answering questions, which includes a discussion of when questions become challenges.

1. Suppose that a student comes to your office and asks about the grade on a test. What would you say to the student?

2. What will you do if a student becomes argumentative about a grade which he/she feels is unfair?

3. What if you make a mistake in grading? What will you do when the student points that out to you?

3. 2. c   Seeking Advice

American students will sometimes ask their instructors for advice about matters that relate not only to their performance in the classroom but to personal matters. The American educational system encourages close interaction between teachers and students in elementary school and to some extent in high school as well. Given their previous experiences, students may ask for advice from a college/university teacher because in their previous experience teachers have been considered caring adults.

Students may want to ask advice about which courses to take or which instructors to take them from. Although it is acceptable for a teacher to advise a student about what courses to take, it is not ethical for a teacher to talk about other teachers except in a positive manner. Students may ask whether another teacher is fair, a hard grader, a good lecturer, and so on. Often they ask for advice about which section or course will be easiest. A skillful teacher avoids making value judgments in response to such requests for advice. It is acceptable for the teacher to explain the requirements for a certain major or course or to recommend a given course as helpful for a student or as one that might be of interest. It is important that the teacher who makes such recommendations also know the requirements of the program or department, so that he/she does not recommend that a student take courses that will not advance the student toward his/her degree. If the teacher is not thoroughly aware of the requirements, it would be preferable to send the student to someone who is.

In the American educational system, undergraduate students choose their majors; they are not selected to study certain fields based on their performance on tests. Consequently, a student may pick a field for which he/she is not truly suited. In such cases, the student may seek the advice of a teacher to know either how to do better in the chosen field or how to select a more appropriate major. Because decisions about one's major determine, for example, which courses a student should take and possibly how long it will take the student to complete a degree, it is imperative that the person giving advice know the options very well. Poor or inaccurate advice may result in the student's not graduating on time or having to take many extra courses. As previously stated, the teacher should not try to give advice unless he/she is qualified to do so.

Sometimes, undergraduates, especially first- and second-year students, find themselves overwhelmed by the large numbers of students in their classes. If they have a class, such as a lab or a discussion group, which is small and in which the teacher has learned their names, they may feel more comfortable going to that teacher than to others because the teacher's calling on them by name makes them feel that the teacher is interested in them as individuals rather than just as numbers or impersonal beings to be taught. Consequently, students are more likely to approach teachers of small classes than those who present the lectures to large classes.

For some American undergraduates, going away to a college or university is their first experience away from home. They may feel lost, especially if they are attending a large university, and they may want someone to talk to about their feelings, for example, of homesickness. Some teachers feel prepared to help students with their personal problems; others do not. Even if the students do not expect the teacher to help, they may expect the teacher to be sympathetic and able to direct them to someone who can help. Thus, it is important to know what is expected of you in your role as teaching assistant and what other resources are available on campus for dealing with student problems. When in doubt, a good rule of thumb is to refer students to the departmental secretary for information.

Assignment

1. How are you expected to handle students who come to you with personal problems?

2. How are you expected to handle students who come to you with academic problems?

3. Is there a learning resource center to help students with academic problems? Where is it located?

4. Who is available on your campus to help students with personal problems? Is there a counseling office? If so, where is it located?

5. Is there a peer counseling service? If so, how can students take advantage of it?

Chapter ◆ 4

Profiles of Teachers in American Colleges and Universities

◆ OVERVIEW

In the American educational system, teachers are expected to interact with students in certain ways, some of which may be different from the ways that teachers interact with students in your culture. Although this chapter presents only a generalized view of how teachers in postsecondary education are expected to act, it may help you to identify appropriate roles for you to fulfill in your position as teaching assistant. Again, it is important for you to remember that each college or university has its own "culture" and that you will need to check with your instructor or some other person who is aware of the culture of the institution that you are now attending to see to what extent the following descriptions are applicable to your situation.

4.1 In the Classroom, Section 1

In American colleges and universities, teachers are expected to perform some duties that may be handled in different ways in other cultures, for example, designing the syllabus or setting examinations. In addition, teachers conduct their classes in ways that may not be expected in other cultures. The teacher often has responsibility for several different duties within a given course. Depending on the particular teaching assignment that he/she has, the teacher may need to act in all or only some of the following roles.

4.1.a Course Designer

In the role of course designer, the teacher is responsible for establishing the rationale for the course and for determining its requirements. This role is usually filled by a senior faculty member or a faculty committee. Also, courses are usually approved or accepted by some central academic body or committee within the institution (e.g., the Academic Planning Committee); once approved, they cannot be changed without the approval of that body.

Assignment

1. What is the procedure for establishing the rationale and requirements for a course in the institution you are now attending?

2. When was the last time there were any changes made in the course that you are assigned to teach?

4.1.b Lecturer

As a lecturer, the faculty member or teaching assistant is expected to present material to a class of students in a fashion that is considered organized, logical, and understandable. In order to do this, the person must know the styles of explanations that are expected and can be comprehended by the students (see 6.1–6.4). Lectures may last from a few minutes (in preparation for a lab, for example) to an hour or more (in the main class for a course).

Assignment

Given your assignment as a teaching assistant, will you be expected to lecture at any time? You might, for example, be asked to present a lecture to a class when your professor is out of town, or maybe your assignment is to provide all of the lectures for the course. Or you might need to present a short lecture each week at the beginning of a lab, explaining or reviewing the theory to be illustrated by the lab. Or you might have to explain or review the procedures to be used in the lab. List any lecturing assignments you might have here.

4.1.c Discussion Leader

Often a large class will break into smaller groups for discussion of the ideas presented in the lecture. Such groups may meet at different times during the week or even during the regular time set aside for the large class. Some teachers like to conduct discussions as part of the regular class. Whatever the setting, the discussion leader has several duties, including defining the task(s) of the groups, asking leading or probing questions, maintaining the discussion, and summarizing at the end of the discussion. (See 3.1.c, Chapter 8, and Chapter 19 for more on discussions.) The purpose of the discussion is to allow the students to ask questions or to raise problems, to demonstrate that they understand, or to explore ideas (rather than having the teacher tell them the answer). Discussion groups are highly interactive and require that the leader have good listening skills as well as good questioning skills.

Assignment

In what situations might you act as a discussion leader? List them here.

4. 1. d Review Session Leader

The review session leader is similar to a discussion leader; but in review sessions the students often ask the questions that need to be discussed, indicating to the review session leader what parts of the material covered in the class they want clarified or need to understand better. Sometimes, a review session leader has a set number of topics to cover—the main points to be covered on a test, for example. Thus it is important for the review session leader to be fully aware of the material that has been presented in the course and to know the aims of the course clearly, in order to focus the review on pertinent items. Often this role is assigned to a teaching assistant, who should have attended the lectures and should know the purposes, aims, and requirements of the course thoroughly.

Assignment

1. In your department, who conducts the review sessions?

2. Is this person required to attend the lectures and/or labs?

3. Will you be expected to conduct review sessions, either for a class that you might be teaching or for a course taught by a faculty member?

4. If so, who will be able to help you determine what needs to be covered in the review session?

4. 1. e Enforcer of Rules

In any teaching role in a classroom setting, the person teaching is expected to enforce certain formal rules of behavior (e.g., no smoking or eating in the classroom) and certain informal rules of behavior that may be expected in a given institution (e.g., whether students are allowed to talk to each other during a lecture or during a review session). Some rules are understood; others are made explicit, usually on the first day of class (e.g., attendance policies may be either understood, because they are the same for all courses in the institution, or announced, because they vary from course to course). To be on the safe side, it is always a good idea to have written policies (or to refer students to standardized written policies) *and* to announce them in class.

Chapter 4 *Profiles of Teachers in American Colleges and Universities*

Assignment

1. What rules will you need to enforce?

2. What rules are set by your department or for the particular course for which you are a teaching assistant?

3. What rules, if any, are you allowed to make? Within what limits?

4. Do the students already know all these rules, or will they be new to the students?

4.1.f Textbook Adopter

Again, the textbook adopter is a role usually assumed by a senior faculty member or a faculty committee. The textbook should reflect the goals of the course and provide adequate information and practice to cover most of the requirements of the course. Sometimes one textbook is chosen for the lecture part of a course and another one is chosen for the lab or practice part of the course. If you are asked to choose a lab text, for example, then you must know the rationale and requirements for the course.

Assignment

1. Who chooses the text(s) for the course(s) for which you will be a teaching assistant?

2. Does your department ask for any input from TAs on the choice of text(s)? If so, when and how?

4.2 In the Classroom, Section 2

4.2.a Dealing With Varieties of Students

Unlike many other cultures, the American culture does not see education as available for only some of its people. Although it is true that not everyone goes to college, it is a strong belief in this culture that anyone who wants to go to a college or university and is willing to work hard enough should have the opportunity to do so. This belief is exemplified by such practices as open-door admissions policies, which state that any student in a given state or other specified geographical area must be admitted to a certain institution. It is also underscored by the financial aid programs administered by institutions, states, and the federal government, which are designed to make it possible for students who do not have much money (or whose families do not) to attend college. This emphasis on access to education is part of the larger American idea that a person can do or be anything he/she wants if the individual is only willing to work hard enough.

The result of this philosophy is that there is a great diversity in the student population in American colleges and universities.

Assignment

1. Often an institution has a concise description of the makeup of its student body. Such a description will include high school grade-point averages, average scores on standardized tests, geographical dis-

tribution, numbers and percentage of students receiving financial aid, ages of students, and number and percentage of minority students. Find out which office in your institution has such information, and ask for a copy.

2. Discuss this information with the other participants in your FTA training course. What are the implications of the types of students at your institution for the teaching you will do?

4. 2. b Teaching Styles

In the same way that students have different learning styles, teachers have different teaching styles. But within a given culture, some styles are considered more appropriate than others.

Assignment

1. Do you think that there is more than one acceptable teaching style? Can you describe the appropriate teaching style(s)?

2. Think about the good and the not-so-good teachers that you have experienced in your life. Discuss these within a small group, and then make a list of the characteristics of both types. Do you think U.S. undergraduates would agree with your list of characteristics? If not, why not?

CHARACTERISTICS OF

GOOD TEACHERS	POOR TEACHERS

3. What are the one or two most serious weaknesses or problems that a teacher can have in your culture? in this culture?

4. What can a teacher do to overcome his/her weaknesses?

5. List your own strengths and weaknesses as a teacher or potential teacher in a U.S. university.

STRENGTHS	WEAKNESSES

6. What do you plan to do to maximize your strengths and minimize your weaknesses in teaching in your present U.S. situation?

4.3 Outside the Classroom

4.3.a Conferences

Teachers may wish to hold conferences with students outside of class. Such conferences allow the teacher to meet with one student or a small group of students, often for the purposes of determining that the students are keeping up with the course, for discussing assignments made in the class, or for answering questions students may have. Conferences are usually held in the teacher's office or a designated meeting room within the department.

Some teachers prefer to schedule conferences with students rather than wait for them to appear during office hours (see 4.3.b). Many students are reluctant to drop by during office hours and need a special invitation, such as that provided by scheduling a conference, to meet with the teacher outside of class. Even in small classes, students may feel that the open invitation to office hours is too nonspecific. Also, some students are intimidated by talking one-on-one to a professor; they may feel somewhat less uncomfortable talking with a teaching assistant, but even then they may be reluctant to admit that they have any questions or problems relating to the course.

In a conference, the teacher may assume some of the same roles used in the classroom (see 4.1), especially those of review session leader, which require asking appropriate questions to determine what it is the students do or do not understand. Students are usually expected to take an active role in the conference (see 3.2). Topics that may be discussed include the student's current grade in the course, help with finding appropriate sources or material for a project (such as a term paper), discussion of variations in the rules (for example, absences or late assignments), and additional explanation of material presented in class.

A conference may be arranged by either the teacher or the student. It is important that both parties be clear about the day, time, and place for the conference, and also the duration (how long the conference can last). Once a student has arranged for a conference or agreed to meet with the teacher for a conference, it is expected that the student will appear at the appropriate time and place or notify the teacher if unable to attend.

It is usually considered good policy to leave the door to your office open, at least partially, during conferences; this is particularly true if the student is of the opposite sex. Some privacy may be desirable, especially if the students might feel embarrassed to have others hear the topic of the conversation (e.g., because they would not want others to know that they did not understand the material or would not like others to know what grade they made on an assignment). Nevertheless, closing the door may imply that something is happening in the office that others should not witness, some inappropriate behavior on the part of the teacher or student or both.

Assignment

1. Is it the policy of your department to have teachers hold regular conferences with students?

2. If yes, are there certain times during the term when those conferences should take place (e.g., during the first few weeks of the term, just after midterm, before the final exam)?

3. How are teachers expected to notify students of conferences (by passing out time sheets on which students sign up or by announcing conference times in class, for example)?

4. If students wish to have a conference, how are they expected to arrange one?

4. 3. b Office Hours

It is usually expected that all teachers, including those who are teaching assistants, will establish certain hours during which they will be available in their offices so that students can contact them. Students expect that the teacher will announce those office hours at the beginning of the term and will be available during those hours at the place designated.

The essential rule for holding successful office hours is to be there. If students do take the initiative to go to the teacher's office, it usually is the result of some mental and emotional preparation on the students' part. If they appear during announced office hours and find the door locked or an empty office with no sign of the teacher, they will certainly be disappointed—and probably angry. So you should consider the announcement of office hours as part of a contract: you agree to be there and to be available to those students who may drop by. If, for some unavoidable reason, you must be gone during office hours, even for a short time, you should put up a sign, indicating when you will be back.

The teacher should be prepared to appear pleased that students have come. A teacher's office is viewed as teacher territory and a somewhat unfriendly place by some students. If the teacher's greeting is brusque, or worse, if there is no greeting, a student will feel even more uncomfortable. Any courteous style of greeting with which the teacher is comfortable will probably be effective. Also, teachers should indicate the amount of time that the student can have, if the time is limited. The teacher might say something like, "Pat, I'm glad you came by. I have to leave for a class in ten minutes, though. Would you like to come in for that amount of time, or would it be better to schedule a time when we'll have more time?" This offers the student the opportunity to get the help needed while indicating that the teacher is interested in the student.

It is important for the teacher to be sure that the student's question or problem is clearly understood before beginning to deal with it. One way to do this is to ask the student questions such as "What can I do for you today?" After the student has explained, the teacher can paraphrase what the student has said (e.g., "So you want to talk about some additional sources for your term paper").

The teacher needs to be able to indicate when the reason that led the student to come may require help of a kind that the teacher cannot provide. Some students may have complaints about things over which the teacher has no control (e.g., departmental attendance policies) or may have personal problems that the teacher does not feel comfortable discussing or does not have the expertise to handle. In such cases, it is important for the teacher to be sympathetic while at the same time indicating that he/she is not prepared to deal with the problem and be able to direct the student to appropriate offices or people to get answers or help. Most teachers are not qualified to deal with the personal problems students may have, nor do they feel comfortable hearing about them; but they should be aware of the services offered on campus from which the student could benefit. Many institutions compile a list of offices and agencies on campus that offer specific sorts of assistance for students (and faculty). You should find or compile such a list, including offices like the counseling center, the student affairs office, the health center, the students' attorney, and so on.

Assignment

1. What kind of message could you put on the door of your office if you had to go to another office or lab for a few minutes during your office hours? Write it here.

2. What message would be appropriate if you found that you could not keep your office hour one day? Write it here.

3. What are some common greetings you might use when students first enter your office?

4. Assume that a student appears at your door just as you are getting ready to leave the office (at the end of the time you have designated for office hours). What would you say to that student?

5. What are some questions you might ask your students in order to help you understand the question or problem that brought the student to your office?

6. Find out if your institution has a list of resources like those previously described. If so, where can you get a copy?

7. If a student needed to get help with personal problems, what could you say to the student to indicate that you are concerned about the student but that you cannot help him/her with a personal problem? (Be sure to indicate who may be able to help and where that person may be found.)

4.3.c Social Occasions

How often students and teachers meet at social occasions depends on the customs at each specific campus and within the particular department. Some departments maintain strict divisions between the various levels—that is, faculty, graduate students, and undergraduates.

Since each institution has its own social culture, and there may be variations within an institution in each department, it is important for each teaching assistant to determine what is considered the appropriate behavior in his/her department. Asking a supervisor or experienced teaching assistants is one way to get the required information; close observation is another.

Often there will be a department social function early in the fall term for all faculty and graduate students, including teaching assistants. This may take the form of a picnic or a coffee hour. The particular kind of event will dictate the level of formality. In some departments, it is the practice for faculty and students (usually graduate students but sometimes also undergraduates) to socialize on Friday afternoons. Some departments have teams of students and faculty entered in local intramural leagues (bowling, softball, etc.). It is important for you to know if attending such activities is expected of you. Often failure to take part in these activities is interpreted as a rejection of the other members of the department. Generally, it is a good idea to figure out some way to take part. If alcohol is served, there also will almost always be soft drinks available as well. If you don't know how to play baseball, you can at least cheer for the team. But if your department views participation of some sort as a sign of cooperation, it is vital for you to be there.

Whatever the social occasion, it may still be expected that students use the titles of faculty (Dr., Professor). In some cases, graduate students may be invited to use the first names of the faculty during informal social occasions; but, even when this is the case, graduate students may also be expected to return to the use of titles in the classroom.

Assignment

1. What social activity occurs in your department at the beginning of the school year, if any?

2. What regular social functions occur in your department (e.g., Christmas party, Friday afternoon social hour, coffee before departmental seminars, etc.)? If you do not know the answers, talk to experienced graduate assistants or your adviser to find them.

3. Which of these activities do you expect to find most unusual or uncomfortable?

4. What can you do to take part in them in a way that is not too uncomfortable for you?

5. What is the accepted practice in your department concerning the use of names and titles at social functions? Are there differences depending on the specific social occasion or the participants (e.g., whether or not undergraduates are in attendance)?

PART·TWO
BACKGROUND TO TEACHING

Chapter ♦ 5

Planning and Organizing the Course

♦ OVERVIEW

Each course in a university curriculum is designed to meet certain goals. For example, such goals include giving students a general understanding of the subject area, presenting basic concepts in the subject area, providing students with an opportunity to learn important techniques necessary for continued study in the field, and so on. The course syllabus reflects the course goals. It is important that everyone involved with the course know and understand those goals; it is not enough to know the material to be covered. Even if you are not involved in setting the goals for the course you will teach, you should be sure that you know what those goals are.

5.1 Setting Goals

In setting goals for a course, the following questions can provide the teacher with guidance:

- What are the most important aspects of the subject matter?
- What skills should be furthered by the course?
- What do students need to be able to do to demonstrate mastery of the subject matter?
- What principles or procedures do the students need to learn?
- What should students have learned by the end of the course?
- How will this course provide a foundation for other courses in the department or work in the field?

After deciding on some general goals for a course, the teacher needs to think about how each will best be achieved—for example, through reading, lecture, discussion, and so on.

Assignment

1. Using the above questions as a guide, list 4–10 general goals for the course you will be assisting in. Consult with your supervisor or an experienced teaching assistant.

2. Which of the goals that you have written is most important? Why?

3. How will you achieve each of these goals?

5.2 Preparing the Course Syllabus

It is important for a teacher, especially a new teacher or one whose command of the language may not be perfect, to plan carefully the course that will be taught. A course outline or syllabus should be written out in detail, including general goals and a weekly or daily schedule of activities. Often, students expect to see such a syllabus on the first day of class. Many institutions or departments require that a course syllabus be provided students during the first week of class.

Find out from your department if you are expected to plan the syllabus for the course. Frequently, teaching assistants teach from a syllabus designed by the regular faculty of the department. In such cases, your responsibility will be for the weekly and daily plans that accomplish the goals set by the departmental syllabus.

Preparing the course syllabus requires the following sequence of activities:

First, after answering questions such as those in 5.1, break down your overall goals into discrete steps or learning objectives. Courses that are tied to a particular textbook will need to be planned around the objectives that are presented in the text and around the order that the text authors recommend. (See 17.1, 17.2 and Chapter 18 for more information on and practice for text-based courses.)

Second, make a schedule for accomplishment of these steps or objectives, working backward from your goals.

Third, decide on the topics for the course and how these will tie in with reading assignments.

Fourth, plan a weekly schedule that includes the course materials, test dates, due dates for assignments, and holidays when the university does not hold class.

Fifth, decide on a daily schedule. Some instructors designate certain days every week for certain activities (e.g., discussions of reading, problem-solving activities, video viewing), while others organize the lesson schedule in essentially the same way each day (e.g., preview activity, questions from reading, lecture, questions about lecture, discussion).

Assignment

1. Get a syllabus from your departmental office for a course similar to the one that you will teach. Analyze the syllabus. What information is included about the course? about the instructor? about rules for student behavior? Compare this syllabus with those brought by the other FTAs.

2. Based on that analysis, determine the information that seems to be required by your institution for a course syllabus.

3. Ask your supervisor or an experienced TA about your department's policy on course syllabi. Are they required? Do they need any departmental approval? Are they kept on file by the department? Is there any written guide for the preparation of the syllabi for your department's courses?

4. If you are planning now for a course that you will soon teach, go through the preceding steps listed to prepare a syllabus for your course. Share that syllabus with the other FTAs to get any needed help in revising it.

5. If you are already teaching a course, bring in the syllabus to share with the other FTAs. Explain the factors that you had to consider while preparing it.

Chapter • 6

Presenting in Class or Lab

◆ OVERVIEW

In order to implement the goals identified for a course, the teacher will be involved in presenting ideas, information, and other kinds of material to students. The teacher is expected not only to know the subject but to be able to present it in ways that make it both *understandable* and *interesting* for students.

Understandable means the subject is explained in language and terms at the level appropriate to the students. To be able to present in an understandable fashion, the teacher must know a lot about the students: what have they learned prior to entering this class? how do they expect teachers to present the material? In addition, the teacher must present material that is correct. Many teachers find that it is easier to be sure that they are correct than that they are understood. No matter how well teachers know the material, they fail in their work as teachers if their students do not understand the content of the class.

Being *interesting* is also important. The best teachers want to get their students interested in and excited about their topic. Most American students indicate that they learn better when the subject is presented in an interesting fashion.

Because these expectations on the part of students may be quite different from what you are used to, this book provides opportunities, in other chapters, for you to think about the differences between high school and undergraduate education in the U.S. and in your home country. It also provides guided observation activities to help you understand how better to communicate with your undergraduate students in helpful ways. This chapter is designed to provide you with an understanding of the expectations in this educational system.

Chapter 6   Presenting in Class or Lab   47

6.1   Types of Explanations

Teachers frequently have the task of explaining things to students. The purpose of an explanation is to make something understandable, but explaining things that one knows well is not always easy. The teacher is obviously more experienced, knows more about the subject, and often has more interest in the subject than the undergraduate students. Planning effective explanations for undergraduates involves analyzing the course content and presenting it in ways to meet their needs. Knowing what their needs are, in turn, requires an understanding of their prior education and their purposes in taking the course.

Researchers have found that college/university teachers generally use three major types of explanations: (1) teachers give definitions of concepts and terms; (2) they describe structures, processes, events, concepts; and (3) they provide reasons for things.

Assignment

Which of the following topics would require a definitional explanation, a descriptive explanation, or a reason-giving explanation? If a description is to be used, what is being described—a process, an event, or an object?

1. What is the meaning of the term *mutagen*?

2. What is a computer?

3. Explain how a bank holding company is organized.

4. Explain how paper is manufactured.

5. Why does clean water freeze at a different temperature from dirty water?

6. Why does your department use graduate teaching assistants?

7. What is a binocular microscope?

8. Why does the earth rotate?

9. What is *zoning*?

10. Describe a Molotov cocktail.

6.2 More Work With Explanations

Work with another student from your field. List as many topics as you can that could be used in explanations that define, describe, and give reasons.

Definitional Explanation Topics

1. What does the *time value of money* mean?
2. _____
3. _____
4. _____
5. _____
6. _____
7. _____
8. _____
9. _____

Descriptive Explanation Topics

1. List the steps in evaluating an investment.
2. Explain the organization of a corporation.
3. Describe the physical setup of the New York Stock Exchange.
4. _____
5. _____
6. _____
7. _____
8. _____
9. _____

Reason-Giving Explanation Topics

1. Why did the Korean economy boom in the 1970s?
2. Justify continued exploration of outer space.
3. _____
4. _____
5. _____
6. _____
7. _____
8. _____
9. _____

6.3 Characteristics of Effective Explainers

Explaining things to undergraduates is difficult for most of those who have moved beyond their level of education, understanding, and even interest. Planning explanations for them involves analyzing the course content and presenting it in ways to meet their needs. Knowing what their needs are requires an understanding of their prior education and their purposes in taking the course. To gain that knowledge, this foreign teaching assistant training course recommends that you think about the differences between high school and undergraduate education in the U.S. and in your home country. It also provides guided observation activities to help you understand how better to communicate with your undergraduate students in helpful ways.

Meeting their needs also requires that you present your explanations in ways that they are accustomed to and can follow. The modes of explanation and communication that you experienced as an undergraduate might not be appropriate for your students. Moreover, the methods being used by your graduate professors are unlikely to be appropriate for these less-experienced students.

There are three aspects to success in teaching. The first of these, knowledge of content, we will leave to you and your academic department. The other two are (a) effective use of spoken language and of gestures to communicate and (b) effective development of appropriate relationships. That is, effective presentation of explanations is much more than just knowing the content.

Speaking

To be able to communicate as a classroom teacher, a non-native speaker of American English must have advanced skills in spoken English. No matter how much a person knows about a topic, he or she cannot communicate that knowledge without advanced language skills. These skills are dealt with in Part Three. In addition, explainers develop specialized uses of spoken English that are thought to be appropriate to the instructional setting. The spoken English used in lecturing is usually different from conversational English in speed, emphasis, length of speaking without interruption, and other features.

Gestures

Most of us are aware that we communicate with our bodies as well as with our words. We have learned that "body language" changes from culture to culture. In order to communicate effectively with your American undergraduates, you will need to learn some American body language. This body language can be used much as you use English—for effective communication in particular contexts. When communicating with people from your own culture, you will, of course, continue to use your native body language.

Eye Contact

An essential feature of the body language of American teachers is the use of eye contact. Looking individual students in the eye indicates several important things to American undergraduates: (1) The teacher recognizes their existence; (2) the teacher is not afraid of them and is relaxed in their presence; (3) the teacher is through writing on the board (or with some other activity) and is ready for class attention again.

Eye contact and head position can communicate meanings that contradict the words of the teacher. Suppose a teacher is looking down at the textbook and only the top of the head can be seen, and the teacher says, "Do you have any questions or comments?" The students are quite sure that the teacher does not really want any questions or comments, especially if the teacher pauses only one or two seconds before continuing to lecture.

Development of Appropriate Relationships

Success as an explainer depends on more than knowledge of content and skill in using language and gestures. The teacher must be able to establish appropriate and effective relationships with students. As you observe American teachers and discuss their behaviors, you will become aware of certain expected classroom interactions between teacher and students. Many effective teachers know the names of their students, even when teaching quite large sections. The teacher uses this knowledge in several ways:

- In taking attendance, the teacher can look at the student while calling his/her name to indicate that the teacher knows the student.
- In answering questions, the teacher can use the student's name to permit the question ("Yes, Susan, do you have a question?") or to answer a spontaneous question ("Sure, Pete, I'll repeat the definition").
- In calling on students to give answers or other information, the teacher can indicate which student should respond by using the student's name.

While some people seem to learn names easily, most teachers have found it necessary to develop methods by which they can quickly learn the names of students during the first few days of the term. To build rapport with your students, you must learn their first names early in the term. The faster you learn them, the more comfortable your students will feel. Experienced teachers recommend these methods: (1) Some teachers like to assign seats alphabetically and then make a seating chart. Since students prefer to sit with their friends, this method can cause some student dissatisfaction, however. (2) Some teachers make a seating chart during the first class and have the students sit in those same places all term. They memorize the names from the chart. (3) Some teachers use memory tricks such as thinking of physical characteristics that they can associate with each name. They may write these characteristics on three-by-five-inch cards below the student's name and use those cards to take attendance. Use whatever method you find most effective to learn students' names.

Teachers also build better relationships with their students when they smile and show enthusiasm for the class. These behaviors indicate to the students that the teacher cares about their learning and enjoys being in their presence.

Courses that include discussion activities (such as case studies) or discussion sections give the explainer additional opportunities for building rapport. Asking the students about their opinions and giving them an opportunity to participate in the discussion are activities that can be used by the teacher to make the students more enthusiastic learners.

You will observe that some successful teachers use the time immediately before and after class for informal contact with students. Students are encouraged to ask questions and to talk about their experiences related to the content of the course. Because the students have found the teacher enthusiastic and helpful in these less formal contacts, the students are more likely to ask questions and to participate in discussions during the class itself.

The relationship between teacher and students is an important and sometimes difficult one. The observation, discussion, and practice given in the foreign teaching assistant training course are designed to help you have effective, rewarding, and appropriate relationships with your American undergraduate students.

Characteristics of Effective Explainers

1. Use of Spoken English
    a. They use relatively short sentences.
    b. They pause in appropriate places.
    c. They vary their rate of speech.
    d. They vary the loudness of their speech.
    e. They talk loudly enough to be heard by all students.
    f. They do not talk too loudly or seem to scream at students.
    g. They make few grammatical errors.
    h. They pronounce key vocabulary correctly.

i. They understand questions from students.
  j. They respond clearly to the students' questions.
2. Use of Body Language
   a. They use emphatic gestures (e.g., hand movements and raised eyebrows).
   b. They gain eye contact with several students while talking.
   c. They regain eye contact after writing on the board or after other activities such as reading from text.
3. Relationship Skills
   a. They call on students by name.
   b. They use the names of students who ask questions.
   c. They show enthusiasm toward the subject matter.
   d. They are courteous and respectful of students.
4. Lecturing Skill
   a. They use good examples.
   b. They clearly state the purpose of the class.
   c. They clearly state the topics being discussed.
   d. They organize lectures, classes, and courses well.
   e. They clearly state the organization for the students.
   f. They present formulas or graphs clearly.
   g. They write key vocabulary on the board or use an overhead transparency.
   h. They use organizing vocabulary to indicate relationships between parts of an explanation.
   i. They answer questions correctly.

Assignment

Working with the other participants in the FTA training course, analyze the list of characteristics of effective explainers. Answer the following questions.

1. What are your reactions to the list based on your prior experience?

2. Is there anything you would like to add to it?

3. Have you observed these behaviors in the classes you have attended or that you have observed?

6.4 Organization of 50-Minute Classes

Classes generally have the same three-part structure that is used in writing English. Your students will better understand your discussion if you use this basic outline to plan and deliver your lectures.

I. Introduction: Getting started—calling roll, getting the students' attention, making announcements, returning papers, telling the students what the class will be about, indicating key concepts or key vocabulary.

II. Body: The presentation or discussion that is the major purpose of the class.

III. Summary or Conclusion: Review of the major features of the content; reminders of announcements or other information given earlier.

You will note in your observation of effective teachers that the ritual is to tell students at the beginning of the class what the goals are for the session, at the end of class to review for students what occurred, and then to indicate what will happen in the next class.

To start the class, the teacher must do something to indicate to the students that it is time to begin. You will observe many different ways of doing this, and you will need to select some that you feel comfortable with. During the introductory period, the teacher calls roll, makes announcements about upcoming tests and due dates, returns test and homework papers, and tells the students the general purposes and outline for the class.

There are many different ways of organizing the body or the central part of the lecture. These differences depend on the central purpose of your course. Generally these will be: (1) to describe a process or event; (2) to explain a thesis; or (3) to compare events, processes, or theses.

For example, your class could be a general introduction to how a computer works intended for a group of undergraduates who have used computers but who do not know how they function. The organization of that class might look like this:

Outline of a Class With a Lecture on How a Computer Works

I. Introduction:
   A. Call roll.
   B. Remind students of the upcoming test; explain types of questions and material to be covered; remind students of the grading system for the course.
   C. Return homework and ask for questions.
   D. Tell students that the class will be about how computers function and explain the outline of the presentation.
      1. This is important because. . . .
      2. First, I'll give some important definitions. . . .
      3. Then, I'll explain how the various parts of the computer interact. . . .

II. Body:
   A. Terminology—(a) words listed on board, (b) technical definitions given, (c) definitions explained, (d) get students to ask questions to be sure they understand.
   B. Relationships among the basic parts of the computer—(a) these are the parts; (b) this is how they relate; (c) so, a computer has these parts and they interact in these set ways.
   C. The process by which a computer computes.

III. Conclusion:
   A. Today, we've gone over some really important terms that you need to learn and talked about the process of computing.
   B. This information is important because. . . .
   C. Next class we'll have the test we talked about earlier. If you have any questions about the test, please talk with me now or make an appointment.

54 Chapter 6 *Presenting in Class or Lab*

Assignment

The teacher of the training course will arrange for you to view a videotape of an undergraduate lecture section. Analyze the lecture in detail. If your instructor plans to show more than one videotaped lecture, you will be asked to make multiple copies of this page.

1. What is the purpose of the class—what kind of presentation is being given?

2. What does the teacher do in the introduction?

3. When does the introduction stop? How can you tell?

4. How is the body of the class organized?

5. How does the teacher involve the students in the class?

6. When does the conclusion start? How can you tell?

7. What does the teacher include in the conclusion?

6.5 Adding Interest Through Associations, Examples, and Humor

The instructor may use real-life examples or humor to break the potential monotony of a straight lecture style. These are methods for making an explanation interesting as well as understandable.

6.5.a Associations and Examples

Whenever possible, an attempt should be made to relate the content of the lesson to students' real-life experiences or interests. An object or an idea can be described in terms of its usefulness in everyday life or can be placed in the context of popular culture. For example, the object or idea can be described in terms of its relationship to a famous figure, the environment, or an important news story. Or, the instructor may be able to describe the object or idea in terms of his or her own personal experience in a way that will make it more concrete and interesting for the students.

6.5.b Humor

Humor can be used to introduce a lesson or a concept in a way that catches the students' interest and attention. There are certain common structures for generating jokes or humor in American culture. The main principle for generating humor is to juxtapose two things in an unlikely way. For instance, humor can be generated by defining something in an unusual way. The following are some examples of humorous classroom definitions created when things are defined according to an unusual or nonprimary function:

- In a computer science class: "A Macintosh is something you give your teacher as insurance."
- In an anatomy class: "The epiglottis is that organ which attempts to keep the windpipes of small children free of pennies, buttons, and earrings."
- In a mathematics class: "A math book is something that makes a serviceable doorstop."

Another way of generating humor is by using standard joke patterns. One of the most common ones in American humor is the following pattern, which juxtaposes an exaggerated situation with an exaggerated result.

"I know a [NOUN] that is so [ADJECTIVE] that [RESULT CLAUSE]."

or simply

"[NOUN] is so [ADJECTIVE] that [RESULT CLAUSE]."

An example of this stereotypical joke pattern is found in the following:

"I know a town that is so small that its zip code is a negative number."

Humor reflects much about the culture and thus what is funny in one culture may not be considered funny in another culture. Telling jokes is not always easy; many people cannot effectively tell jokes in their first language, let alone in a second language. Before you tell a joke in class, it would be a good idea to practice it on a friend or acquaintance who is a native American English speaker.

Some subjects are not considered appropriate for classroom humor. These include references to the students' ability to learn, to physical characteristics of the students, or student attempts at learning or understanding the material. It is safer to use the course material or other topics that do not directly relate to students as the subject for jokes. You also may make impersonal jokes about yourself, if you feel comfortable doing that, as long as these jokes do not have the effect of undermining your authority.

56 Chapter 6 *Presenting in Class or Lab*

Assignment

1. Working with one or more course participants, try to develop real-life associations, examples, or humorous definitions for each of the following:

    a chemical element or compound

    a famous mathematical formula

    a physical law

    a principle of economics

2. Working alone or with other course participants, try to make up jokes on the following pattern:

    "This book/class/lesson is so hard/easy/interesting/essential that. . . ."

6. 6 Adding Variety to Class Formats

1. Classes may be teacher-centered or learner-centered. In a teacher-centered lesson, the teacher usually stands at the front of the room and directs remarks to an audience of students. To maintain this type of communication, the teacher has to be skilled in presenting information clearly and in an interesting manner that will be understandable to the students and can hold everyone's attention.

    a. What are some ways in which the teacher can present information in a clear but interesting manner?

    b. What are the characteristics of an interesting presentation?

2. Varying the style of presentation by using a combination of visual information, lecture, and other types of audio information such as tape recordings can ensure a high interest level in a teacher-fronted class.

a. Can you think of ways in which audiotapes might enhance a presentation in your subject area?

b. What about overhead projections or videotape?

3. Maintaining eye contact is also important in teacher-fronted lectures. Be careful not to "talk to" the chalkboard or the book.

   a. What are some of the ways that you can maintain eye contact with the audience, instead of "talking to" the chalkboard or the screen when using an overhead projector?

   b. What are some ways to establish eye contact with the audience if you are reading from a book or other printed material?

4. In a learner-centered mode, the teacher plans the lesson so that students will play an active role in the content of the lesson. The teacher may assign activities for students to perform in groups or may allow students to direct the course of a lesson loosely planned to cover a certain reading or subtopic of the course. Or, the instructor may assign individual students to prepare certain parts of the lesson that they will present to the class. In the latter case, a student or students take on the role of teacher. In some disciplines, however, it is not acceptable for the teacher to operate in a learner-centered mode, at least not often.

   a. In your department, is it an accepted practice for the teacher to have students perform in groups or present parts of the lesson to the rest of the class?

   b. To what extent is it accepted for students to act in teacher roles (give information, clarify, direct the discussion, etc.)? Under what circumstances is it accepted?

   c. Discuss with other participants ways in which variety can be added to the following classes.
      - an introduction to organic or general chemistry
      - a class in trigonometry
      - an ancient history class
      - a beginning physics class
      - a microeconomics class

Before you use any of the suggestions your group discusses, check for the appropriateness of those activities in your department.

6.7 Nonverbal Communication

In American culture, one's "body language," or nonverbal communication, is often as important as the verbal content in getting a message across to an audience. Americans use many kinds of nonverbal signals—such as gestures, body posture, and movement—to enhance their communication with an audience, whether that audience is one person in a private conversation or an auditorium of several hundred. Use of gestures, body posture, and movement can greatly enhance your communication skills as a teaching assistant when lecturing to a class, conducting discussions, or meeting with students during office hours.

Americans like to have a lot of different kinds of clues to the speaker's mood and intentions. Facial expressions, hand gestures, body posture, and movement can provide these desirable signals. To speak effectively in an American cultural context, one needs to use these several channels of communication simultaneously. In some cultures where gestures are much more subtle, this much information would be considered unnatural for a speaker and distracting for a listener. Thus, many non-native speakers will have to learn new skills for building nonverbal communication into their teaching repertoire in order to improve the chances of succeeding in communication with an audience of American students.

Facial Expressions

It is common for Americans to raise the eyebrows to emphasize a point while speaking. Raised eyebrows often accompany raised intonation as well. Sometimes, when another person is speaking, an American will raise the eyebrows to indicate special interest in what the other person is saying. In other cases, the listener's raised eyebrows indicate doubt, surprise, or disagreement regarding the speaker's words.

Americans will often show their attitude by either smiling or frowning openly. When speaking in front of a group, it is common for a person to smile periodically as a way to maintain good feelings with the audience. Frowning indicates various kinds of negative attitudes such as anger, distrust, or confusion, and so this expression should be avoided when lecturing. Americans will often interpret an expressionless face as signifying lack of ideas, feelings, or interest, though the tone of voice or gestures that the speaker uses can compensate to some extent for a face that Americans find hard to read.

One of the most important social signals is eye contact. Americans prefer to establish eye contact with different members of the audience for several seconds each, moving the gaze around the room. A shorter period of eye contact or lack of eye contact will indicate nervousness, shyness, or lack of confidence to some Americans, while a prolonged gaze may indicate threat or aggression. When speaking from notes, you will have a better chance of keeping your audience members' attention if you establish eye contact periodically.

Hand Gestures

It is quite common for Americans to use many types of hand gestures to accompany speech. Here are some common and useful hand gestures:

- The index finger pointing up in the air: This gesture is used to underscore an idea, to make a point strongly.

- A raised and closed fist striking into the air: This is a forceful gesture, which accompanies very strong statements, especially those known by the speaker to be controversial or expected by the speaker to meet some resistance.

- The two palms face open to the audience at about waist height, the arms bent at the elbow and held close in at the sides of the body: This is an indication of the speaker's openness, vulnerability, or willingness to share something—for example, an idea or a feeling—with the audience.

- The two hands open, palms facing toward the chest, rotating around each other in a circular motion: This is a gesture used to indicate the unfolding of ideas. It is used to emphasize or underscore remarks. It may indicate that the ideas being expressed are being generated as the person is speaking, rather than having been preconceived.

- The alternate overturning of the left and then the right palm, with the arms held closely at the sides and bent up at the elbows: This is a common accompaniment of alternative expressions such as *either . . . or* and especially *on the one hand . . . on the other hand.*

Other Gestures

- A single head nod: This gesture indicates agreement or can accompany a stressed word.
- Moving the head to one side: this gesture can indicate questioning behavior and can accompany a word such as *well* used to preface a statement of reservation about a preceding remark.
- Moving the head first to one side and then to the other: This gesture can accompany alternative statements such as *either . . . or* or *on the one hand . . . on the other hand.*
- Shrugging the shoulders: This gesture often accompanies the expression *I don't know* or can substitute for this expression.
- Folded arms: A way to indicate authority or lack of openness to other people or their ideas.

Body Posture

A speaker who stands straight with the legs slightly apart gives the impression of being confident and relaxed. When sitting in a chair, American instructors will assume a comfortable position, usually with the legs together, sometimes crossed at the knees or ankles. The distance from another speaker that is comfortable for most Americans in most nonintimate situations of interaction is two feet or more. Positioning one's body closer than this to an American will often cause that person to back away to a distance that feels more comfortable.

Movement

A lecture can be enhanced by having the speaker move about while speaking. A lecturer should not be fixed, like a piece of furniture, in one place, but rather should be a body that attracts attention through planned movement. At the same time, movement can be overdone, and a speaker who moves too much can appear like a trapped animal, darting from one hiding place or resting place to the next. A lecturer might heighten attention by moving occasionally back and forth from a podium to the board or to an overhead projector. Or the lecturer might go into the audience or step in front of the podium for part of a speech. During group work in a class, the instructor might circulate around the room. In some cases, it might not be possible or appropriate for a speaker to move very far from a particular spot, especially if using a microphone. Even in these cases, however, moving for part of the lecture a bit to the side of the podium or table where one is lecturing can add some attention and interest on the part of the audience. Such movement should occur to be appropriately coordinated with the content of the lecture, because students expect that main points will be signaled by the instructor's body language.

As in other cultures, touching the face or the body with the fingers is considered distracting and a sign of lack of control and sophistication as a speaker.

Assignment

When you see yourself on videotape, watch for your use of body language and notice the ways in which your nonverbal communication complements or interferes with the message of your words. Discuss your observations with the instructor of your FTA training course.

6. 8. Asking and Answering Questions

There are many ways to ask questions in English. Questions beginning with a verb are commonly referred to as *yes/no* questions. If a student asks a *yes/no* question, he/she is often expecting more than a simple *yes* or *no* answer. The *yes/no* question is often intended as an opener or probe to indicate that the questioner would like more information. For example, a student who asks whether the instructor holds a certain opinion is very likely asking the instructor to discuss reasons for holding one as against another point of view.

Sentences in question form beginning with *would you* or *could you* are especially polite. However, it is common for students to ask questions directly and less formally.

Questions beginning with words such as *when, where, how, what kind,* and so on, ask for certain types of information; the opening word acts as a signal to the instructor regarding the type of information that is wanted in the answer. Sometimes, however, an explicit question word may signal specific though less obvious linguistic functions. For example, the following types of questions often are used to indicate skepticism about the proposition expressed after *that*.

> *How is it that. . . ? How can it be that. . . ?*
> *Why is it that. . . ? Why do you think that. . . ?*

Rising intonation can also be used to signal a question. Extra-high intonation throughout or contrastive intonation on a particular word or phrase is a signal of disbelief. For example, if a student asks, "WHEN did you say that radium was discovered?" the contrastive intonation on *when* may indicate that the student thinks you have made a mistake in the date given for the discovery of radium. (See Chapters 12 and 14 for practice with stress and intonation.)

U.S. students are accustomed to asking questions whenever they arise, rather than waiting until the end of the lecture. It is acceptable to ask students to hold questions other than requests for clarification until the end of the period, though it is more common to allow students to ask questions periodically during a lesson. Many instructors solicit questions two or three times within a given class period, at points in the presentation when the instructor has finished one major idea and is ready to begin another one.

To ensure that everyone understands the lesson, it is a good idea to solicit questions not only from those who volunteer them, but also from the quieter students, perhaps calling on them by name. Or, the instructor may call on individual students to answer questions about the content of the lecture, to ensure that they have understood it.

Sometimes students ask questions in a very direct way. Often, however, the intent or even the fact of the question may not be entirely clear. In such cases, the instructor may indicate a lack of understanding and ask for clarification by phrases such as: "I'm sorry, but I'm not sure that I understood your question. Could you elaborate on/paraphrase/explain/clarify your point?"

Other times, students ask questions in ways that do not sound like questions. For example, a student may say "But I thought that. . . ." Or maybe "So if I substitute A into B, I'll get the answer." These types of questions sound like statements, but they serve the function of questions that are intended to clarify what the student thinks he/she understands about the subject. You need to learn to recognize these types of questions.

If a student continually interrupts the lesson by asking questions, the instructor may ask the student to hold any questions until the end of the period or to make an appointment to see the professor.

As the teacher, you will find questions useful, too. You can use them for checking on the understanding of the students and as a method for involving the students in a discussion.

Assignment

1. Observe a section of the class you will probably teach and identify the types of questions that the students ask. Use the "Reference Guide to Question Structures" and "Reference Guide to Question Types" (6.9, 6.10) to guide your identification of question types.

2. Plan a discussion on a section of a text that you are teaching. What types of questions can you use to guide the students?

6.9 A Reference Guide to Question Structures

Questions may be used for different reasons—to seek information, to clarify what someone else said, to confirm what the speaker thinks another person said. Not all questions sound like questions. The following presents structures and purposes of questions often used in classrooms.

Instructors' Question Structures

1. Question word order (often with rising intonation): This is probably the most familiar question type. It includes the questions that begin with verbs ("Are there any questions?") as well as the *wh-* words (*when, where, why, what kind,* and *how*). As you will observe, questions can be addressed either to the class as a whole or to an individual student.

2. Imperative sentence: This question form is less polite than those beginning with verbs or *wh-* words. It is acceptable for the teacher to use this type in seeking information from students; it is not usually acceptable for the students to use in seeking information from the teacher.

    "Tell me why we use this formula." "Give me three examples."

3. Incomplete statement: The teacher begins a statement and then pauses, waiting for one of the students to complete the statement. Sometimes the teacher may indicate a particular student to answer; if the teacher does not do that, anyone in the class may be expected to answer.

    "The third reason is. . . ."

4. Purposefully incorrect statement: A teacher might say, "The formula for water is HO_2." This is a hidden question ("What is the correct formula for water?"). If the teacher uses this device, it is expected that the students will correct the teacher; that is not considered rude behavior, as long as the students do it in a polite manner.

5. Statement word order with rising intonation: In this type, the only clue that this is not a statement, as the word order would indicate, is the rising intonation.

    "This is the correct answer?"

6. Direct eye contact: Sometimes the teacher may use one of the question types above and indicate which student is to answer by looking directly at that student for several seconds. That is a signal that the student should respond, even though the teacher may not have called the student by name.

Students' Question Structures

1. Question order (often with rising intonation): Again, this is the most obvious type. Samples include: "Will you please explain problem 18?" "When will the test be?" "Why do we have to show all our work on our homework problems?" "Is this the only application for that concept?"

2. "I don't understand (*student specifies problem area*)." Although this sounds like a statement, it is really an information-seeking question. Restated, it becomes "Will you explain. . . ?" This question structure is used when the student thinks he/she knows what it is that needs to be explained.

3. Indication of confusion: Again, these sound like statements; but they are, in fact, hidden questions. They could be translated into questions like "Will you explain that again?" "How did you reach that conclusion?" "Could you start from the beginning and go through it all again?" This type of question structure is used by students who are not sure exactly what it is they do not understand; they are so confused that they cannot even identify what they need to know.

    "I'm lost." "I don't know what's going on." "I can't follow this."

4. Extending meaning: In this type of hidden question, the student is asking for confirmation that he/she understands by applying or extending the information given previously.

> *"Then, if I apply this theory to that situation, _____."*

5. Comparison/Contrast: This is another type of hidden confirmation question, asking "Do I understand this correctly?"

> *"That's like the example in the book." "But in another class the professor said _____."*

6.10 A Reference Guide to Question Types

Questions may be used for a variety of purposes. This guide describes the four most common uses of questions in classroom settings.

1. Rhetorical questions

These use question word order and usually have rising intonation, though not always. The teacher uses rhetorical questions to focus the students' attention on the information to be presented next or on the organization of the presentation. But the teacher does not expect that the students will answer the question. Some examples are given below:

> *"So what should I do now that I have determined the number of variables?"* (The teacher continues, answering the question.)

> *"Is that all that we need to know?"* (The teacher continues after a brief pause.) "No, it isn't. We also need to know _____."

2. Information-seeking questions

This type of question is used to elicit information from the students. That information may be some specific detail about the subject, or it may be that the information being sought is whether or not the students understand the material. Information-seeking questions may use any of the question structures given in the Reference Guide to Question Structures (6.9). Some examples are given below:

> *"What is the formula for water?"*
>
> *"Why is it important to check the temperature first?"*
>
> *"The heat is turned off when. . . ."*

3. Clarifying questions

Often it is necessary for the teacher or students to ask questions in an effort to make sure that they understand what the other has said. Clarifying questions can use any of the question structures given in the Reference Guide to Question Structures (6.9). Some examples follow:

Students' Clarifying Questions:

> *"Do you mean that this is the same kind of problem that we had yesterday?"*
>
> *"I'm not sure that I understand what that term means."*

Teachers' Clarifying Questions:

In the same way that your students may have difficulty understanding the way you speak English, you may find that you cannot always understand what your students say, particularly if they speak with a regional accent with which you are unfamiliar. If you cannot understand what the student is saying, then it is impossible for you to respond appropriately. The following sample question structures are some that you can use to clarify what the student is saying.

"I'm sorry, but I didn't hear all of that. Could you repeat it, please."

"Could you restate that for me, please?"

"I'm sorry, but I don't understand your question." (Someone else in the class may act as an interpreter at this point.)

"Show me on the board (in the book, in your notes) *the part you are having trouble with."*

4. Confirming questions

When one speaker thinks he/she understands what another one has said but is not certain, a confirming question may be used. Again, the structure of the question may be of any type. But the purpose is always to indicate that the speaker thinks he/she has understood. Some examples are given below:

Students' Confirming Questions:

"Then if I continue in this fashion, I will be able to get the correct answer." (This may or may not have rising intonation at the end.)

"So, if I miss the test, there won't be a makeup exam and I will just lose a grade, huh?"

Teachers' Confirming Questions:

It is important to be sure that you understand what the student wants before you answer. If you do not understand the question correctly, you may give an answer that will not satisfy the student, which in fact may only frustrate the student. The sample question structures below are some that you can use to clarify what it is you think the student wants to ask.

"You want me to go through this problem again." (The teacher states what he/she heard.)

"You want to know about _____." (The teacher states the part he/she understood and then lets the student complete the rest. Or the teacher fills in the blank and then gives the student the opportunity to indicate that what the teacher thought he/she understood is not what the student meant.)

"So you are asking _____." (The teacher rewords [as opposed to repeats] what he/she thinks the question is.)

Chapter • 7
Using Audiovisual Aids

◆ OVERVIEW

University instructors often use audiovisual aids to supplement the spoken words of their explanations. Using these devices, the instructor can give spellings for important terminology, illustrate a process, and add interest to the explanation through the use of visual stimulation. These aids can be especially useful for foreign teaching assistants as a method of compensation for possible weaknesses in spoken English skills.

7.1 The Chalkboard

The audiovisual aid most commonly used by U.S. teachers is the chalkboard (or *blackboard* or *board*). Foreign teaching assistants need to learn to use this resource well for two reasons: (1) U.S. students expect to gain important information from the materials written on the board; (2) effective use of the board can compensate for problems in spoken English. The following are some suggestions for using the board effectively.

Write clearly and legibly. Generally, teachers use a printed rather than a cursive writing style on the board. You must learn to write in letters that are large enough and dark enough for all your students to read. Practice this by going to a classroom and writing a few sentences and formulas on the board. Then go to the back of the room to see if you can read them.

Plan an organized use of the space. Many foreign teaching assistants have found the following plan effective: Put a general title for the class in the middle of the board—up high so that it is out of the way. Put a brief outline of the class high up on one side of the board and a list of key vocabulary (and words that you have trouble pronouncing) up high on the other side of the board. You can refer to the outline as the class proceeds to help the students understand what is going on. You can point to the vocabulary as it is used to help the students get the correct spelling of these important words and to be sure that they understand what you are saying.

The following illustration shows a method for organizing material on the board that many teachers find effective. The title of the lecture is written in the middle—and left on the board for the entire class period. A list of important words that will be defined or used repeatedly is given on the left side of the board. On the right side, a brief outline of the class is given that can be referred to at transition points to help students follow the lecture. The teacher can use the rest of the space to add additional materials during the presentation of the lecture.

List of key vocabulary and words that are difficult to pronounce	Title	Outline I. II. III. IV.

Do not use unexplained initials or abbreviations. Remember that a major function of an introductory course is to explain basic terminology. Thus, you cannot expect the students to know these words yet. If initials are commonly used in your field rather than the full form, be sure that the students understand the full form and its relationship to the initials.

Keep the materials on the board neat by erasing as you go along. When you get to class, start with a clean board. Then as you work, erase materials that you have finished with before going on to other things. It is good practice to ask students if they are finished with a section of the board before erasing it. Erase the board before you leave the room so that the next teacher starts with a clean surface.

Give the students time to write down what you have written. Before erasing the board, you should ask the class questions such as "Do you have this?" or "Do you need more time to write this?" or "Can I erase this now?"

Avoid talking with your back to the class. When you are writing on the board, you need to develop a method that keeps you facing the students while you talk. If you talk with your face to the board and your back to the class, two things happen: First, your voice is more difficult to hear, which cuts down on comprehensibility; second, you lose eye contact with the students, so that your ability to communicate is lessened. We call this "talking to the board"—which means not talking to the students.

You have two choices to deal with this common problem: (1) You can write first and then turn to talk with the students. This method is best reserved for writing brief passages because Americans are made uncomfortable by long stretches of silence. (2) You can stand at an angle as you write so that you have some eye contact as you talk about what you are doing. If it is necessary to write longer passages, you should narrate what you are doing as you write. When you finish, turn to the class, establish eye contact, and then point out the important parts of what you wrote. If you have long periods of silence as you write, students may began to talk to each other. If you do not establish eye contact often, you give the students a nonverbal signal that they do not have to pay attention or to listen—and so they take their minds off you. A combination of narrating, standing at an angle, and periodically establishing eye contact works well for many teachers.

Assignment

View a videotape of yourself giving an explanation. Make at least one additional copy of this page to use in exercise 3.

1. How well did you use the board? What suggestions do you have for yourself to improve this part of your presentation?

2. Make an exact copy of what was written on the board when the presentation ended.

```
┌─────────────────────────────────────────────────────────┐
│                                                         │
│                                                         │
│                                                         │
│                                                         │
│                                                         │
│                                                         │
│                                                         │
│                                                         │
└─────────────────────────────────────────────────────────┘
```

   a. What did the board look like?

   b. Was it empty? Why?

   c. Was it cluttered? Why?

   d. Were there any mistakes or misspellings? List them here.
   _____
   _____
   _____
   _____

3. After you have practiced giving explanations, view another videotape of yourself giving an explanation. Use a copy of this sheet and evaluate your performance. Do you see any differences between your presentations? What are they?

7.2 The Overhead Projector

In some academic disciplines, such as business administration, statistics, and economics, teachers like to use the overhead projector to show students materials that were prepared before the class. In other disciplines, such as mathematics, teachers usually prefer to use the board to write out materials as a demonstration to students of the ways in which certain problems are handled.

Before deciding to use any educational technology, you should find out if that style of teaching is approved of in your discipline and in your department.

If you wish to use the overhead projector effectively, consider these suggestions:

Prepare transparencies that are easy to read. You should limit the amount of material that is on any one transparency to two or three major points—or to one major point with two or three subdivisions. Or you might have one chart or diagram per transparency. If possible, prepare transparencies from printed or typed material. If you must write the materials by hand, learn to use a clear writing style. To see if your materials are readable, project a transparency and then go to the back of the classroom to find out what your students can actually see. In some cases, large screen projection is available for overhead transparencies, so that a smaller print can be used or so that a larger audience can see the projected image.

Get to class early to be sure that the projector has been delivered and is working. It is very frustrating and embarrassing to have planned a class around overhead materials and then to find that you do not have a projector or that the projector is not working. If this should happen, you may have to use the chalkboard (see 7.1 for suggestions).

Decide if the lights should be turned off. In theory, you are supposed to leave the lights on in the classroom while using the overhead projector so that the students can see to make notes. In some rooms, you will need to turn off the lights (or perhaps just the lights in the front of the room) so that the projected materials can be read easily. Ask the students if they can see so that you can make necessary adjustments.

Do not turn your back to the class. As with effective use of the chalkboard, teachers should avoid turning their backs to the class while using the overhead projector. The students look at the projected image while the teacher looks at the transparency itself. This keeps the teacher facing the class and also makes it possible at the same time to write on the transparency or to point easily to particular sections. It is also important to position yourself so that you do not block the view of any of the students. You should always have an erasable marker (black or dark blue for maximum visibility) for writing on the transparency so that you can add information as necessary. In fact, one possible use of the overhead is to have part of the information already written on the transparency and add the rest as you talk about it during class. Gradually adding information in this way increases the dramatic impact of a presentation and also allows for gradual absorption of material by the audience.

Control the students' attention by using the "revelation" method. One problem in using a transparency is control of what information the students are looking at. That is, you can be talking about the top of the transparency while they are looking at the middle or bottom. You can control what they see by putting a piece of paper over the parts of the transparency that you want to conceal and only gradually revealing the other parts.

Develop a storage and filing system. Many departments have their own machines to make transparencies from photocopies or from originals written in the correct types of ink or pencil. If your department does not have such equipment, your university might have a centralized educational media center that can help you make transparencies. Many copy centers also will make transparencies—for a charge, of course. In any case, making a transparency takes time and energy. Therefore, it is strongly recommended that you develop a storage and filing system for these materials so that they are easily available when you teach the course again—or for other courses or presentations. Be sure to store transparencies in a dark place, as continual exposure to bright light may cause discoloration.

7.3 Other Types of Audiovisual Aids

It is frequently a good technique to use a variety of audiovisual aids in the same class. For example, you can use the overhead projector for some materials and the chalkboard for others.

A class can be greatly improved by the use of audiovisual aids. Not only do such aids help to break up the monotony of listening to a teacher talk for long periods of time, but they often add significantly to the students' understanding of a subject by providing new kinds of input (e.g., visual, through slides, charts, or drawings).

There is a wide range of audiovisual aids that are generally at the disposal of college and university teachers. These include mimeographed or photocopied handouts, overhead projectors, opaque projectors, slide projectors, chalkboards, flipcharts, tape players, and video players.

Audiovisual aids can be used to reinforce concepts already introduced (e.g., through a visual representation of information contained in the lecture) or to supplement the lecture (e.g., by giving additional information not included in the lecture). An overhead projection of a table can provide data to help substantiate a general claim; a diagram can show the functional relationships of the parts of a mechanism or process; the use of an instrument can be demonstrated in front of the class. Cassette tapes, slides, videos, and films relating to different fields of study are often available to borrow or rent through the campus media center. If you want to make your own audiovisuals, most colleges and universities provide consultants and services through the learning-resources or media center to help you make high-quality audiovisual aids.

Assignment

Consider the use of media that would be appropriate to your field, to your teaching assistant assignment, and to the expectations of your students. Give two examples each of uses of the following media:

slides

_____

_____

overhead projections

_____

_____

tape recordings

_____

_____

video recordings

_____

_____

Chapter ♦ 8

Leading a Discussion

♦ **OVERVIEW**

An explanation presents and clarifies information while developing student interest in the topic. A discussion session focuses on developing other student skills. Students learn to present their ideas, experiences, and information clearly and effectively. They learn to interact with other students and with the teacher in academically appropriate ways. They learn to develop and modify their ideas in the face of disagreement and counterevidence. Thus, discussions are less focused on getting the right answer to a question and more concerned with developing the academic and intellectual skills of the students.

Since American students, like most human beings, enjoy talking, well-led discussions can be the most popular part of courses. When observing classes, notice how the rest of the class frequently acts more interested and more involved when fellow students are talking than when the teacher is lecturing.

To get students involved in a discussion requires particular skills and discipline of the teacher. The skills are those of guiding a group so that many different individuals have opportunities to participate in the discussion. The required discipline is not to take over and talk too much yourself. The minute that the teacher starts giving all the answers, the discussion dies.

8.1 Methods for Setting the Stage for a Discussion

Some teachers have found that students are more willing to participate in discussions if they think the teacher is genuinely interested in them and their opinions. One method for establishing this relationship is to use the preclass time effectively. You will frequently find that the students who talk with you about the course prior to class can be depended on to participate in discussions.

American students are accustomed to being asked to participate in discussions. They are usually eager to give their opinions, if they think you really want to hear them. They are also accustomed to having part of the course grade based on participation in class discussions.

Observant teachers soon learn who their better students are. One method for getting a discussion going is to start with a question for one good student. Then turn to another good student and ask for additional information or another opinion.

Always have a complete analysis of the case study or the discussion question in mind. Have some notes made of the major answers. But do not rush in and give your answers. Try to get the students to come up with the information themselves. You might also find that they have additional information and interpretations that you had not thought of that can enhance your understanding of the topic.

Some teachers get students to fill out information sheets at the beginning of each term. In addition to name, address, phone number, and class level, these teachers ask for information on work experience, travel experience, hobbies, and reasons for taking the course. This information can be useful in planning discussions. For example, if the discussion is about the planning process in management of businesses, a student who works for Sears or for IBM might have information about how that corporation's planning processes work.

Assignment

1. Discuss with the members of the FTA training course your observation notes on discussion sessions in classes you have observed. How did the teacher guide the discussion? How many students participated? What kinds of questions were asked? How long did the discussion last? Was the discussion based on materials from the textbook?

2. Using a textbook from a class that you are likely to teach, plan a short discussion (15–20 minutes) based on a discussion activity suggested by the authors of the text. What major points should be made in the discussion? What evidence should the students be able to give for their ideas? What questions can you ask to guide the discussion?

Chapter ♦ 9

Preparing Tests, Grading, and Record Keeping

♦ OVERVIEW

American students, like their counterparts around the world, are concerned with the ways in which they are evaluated in their courses. Also, because they are often vocal about what they expect from their teachers, American students may challenge the teacher about such matters as the appropriateness (or "fairness") of test questions, the methods of grading tests and other work, and the degree to which the teacher's records reflect the student's performance.

Therefore, it is important for you to recognize your responsibilities in these matters. This chapter explains the expectations that students have and how you can effectively meet those expectations as well as uphold the policies of the department and university in which you are teaching.

♦ EVALUATING STUDENT WORK

9.1 Preparing Tests

9.1.a Writing Test Questions

Some graduate teaching assistants are required to prepare some or all of the questions for a test in the course. There are some important guidelines to keep in mind in writing test questions.

First, the questions need to be clear and unambiguous. The student should be able to understand the question easily and not have to guess at what the question asks him/her to do. If the question is not clear, the student may interpret it to mean something other than what the teacher meant and then answer it incorrectly. For example, a question that says, "What did the author say about capital punishment? Do you agree?" seems to ask only for a summary followed by yes or no. If it was intended that the student also comment on the argument presented in the writing or explain why he/she agrees or disagrees, then the question needs to include a statement such as "Explain why you agree or disagree." Similarly, a problem question with the instructions "Solve for the value of x" would seem to indicate that the students can use any method of solution they wish. If it is the intention of the question to find out if the students can use a particular method of solution, then that needs to be stated in the instructions, for example, "Using the graphic method, solve for x."

Second, the questions should focus on the main points in the material to be covered, not on small or insignificant details. This means that the question writer needs to recognize the main points to be covered in the test.

Third, the questions should test material that has been taught. It is unfair to students to test them on material that was not covered in the course, unless that material is considered a necessary prerequisite for the course. For example, some physics course descriptions state that the student must know calculus in order to take the course; in that case, writing a test question that requires the use of calculus in the solution of the problem would be fair. But if the course description specifies that the course does not require calculus as a prerequisite, it would be unfair to write a test question that requires its use.

Sometimes, the course syllabus will state that students are expected to read certain material outside of class and that they will be tested on that material even though it will not be discussed in class. In that case, test questions on that material can be considered fair, if they test the students' knowledge and understanding of the main points of the material.

Assignment

1. Write three questions for a test in an introductory course in your field of study.
   a. _____
   _____
   b. _____
   _____
   c. _____
   _____

2. Share your questions with others in your class, preferably students who are in a different field of study. Did the other students understand the questions? If not, what caused them problems in understanding?

3. Use a textbook in your field and read the questions or problems at the end of any chapter. Find a question that could be interpreted in more than one way. Explain the various meanings to the other participants in the FTA training course.

4. How could you rewrite the question so that it is clear and unambiguous?

9.1.b Relation of Test Material to the Course

It is expected that the material on the test will relate to the major objectives of the course. That is, if the course is a skills course, such as a laboratory course, it is expected that the test will allow students to show that they have developed laboratory skills. Thus a test that requires students to actually use those skills would be appropriate. Similarly, in a mathematics course, the test questions should test the students' ability to use certain mathematical concepts, not their ability to memorize the solutions to certain problems. On the other hand, memorizing certain formulas may be expected for students taking a test in physics, engineering, and so on—perhaps in addition to their being able to use those formulas in actually solving problems.

Students expect that the material on the test will be in some way familiar to them. That is, the problems may be like (though not identical to) problems that were solved in class or assigned for homework. It is not good test practice to ask students to do something on a test that they have not done before. (Such questions may be used on aptitude tests, perhaps, but not on classroom tests.)

Students also expect that they will be given some clues of what to expect on the test. In fact, they may ask the teacher, "What will be on the test?" This question should be interpreted to mean what kinds of material will be covered, not what the specific questions will be (although some students may try to get the teacher to tell them the specific questions). While they should be able to recognize from the lectures, discussions, and labs what the important ideas and concepts in the course are, they still often expect that the teacher will give them some hints about what to expect on the test. If questions on the test seem to them not to have an obvious relation to the material that was covered in the class, they will feel that they are being tricked and that the questions are unfair. This is because they have been taught to expect that the questions will relate to the assigned material.

Important ideas should have been stressed in the lecture or discussion in the class and should have been part of the homework assignments. Then those same ideas or concepts should be tested. If material that was not presented in the class, discussion, lab, or homework appears on the test, the students will feel that those questions are unfair.

9.1.c Determining and Maintaining Department Standards

Many departments have certain policies and standards concerning tests. It is important for you to know exactly what those are and to be certain that you adhere to them. For example, in some departments it is expected that all tests will be written in special examination books (called *blue books*) rather than on notebook paper. In others, it is the policy to give a mass exam to all students in the various sections of a given course, for example, all the students in all sections of beginning biology. Or in a mathematics class, it may be the policy that students have to show all of their work. Or it may be a policy to require all students to take final exams, no matter what their grade may be, whereas in another department only those students with grades below "A" at examination time will be required to take the final exam.

Sometimes it is a departmental or course policy that only certain types of test questions will be given. For example, in a language class, it may be that all questions should be written so that they demand answers written in complete sentences. Or, in a mathematics class, it may be expected that all of the questions will be problem questions (which require students to solve problems or to prove theorems) and that there will be no definition questions. It is important to know about such policies, if you are expected to write any of the test questions.

In some cases, there are no written policies about testing, but there are certain traditions concerning the types of tests that are given. For example, in some colleges or universities it is the tradition that test questions in a mathematics course will always be similar to problems assigned for homework. In other places, the tradition may be always to have at least one extra-credit problem or question (i.e., a problem that can be solved to achieve additional points toward the exam grade) on each test.

Assignment

1. What policies does your department have about the giving of tests? Ask your supervisor or experienced TAs if there are no written policies; if there are written policies, get a copy of them. Write the most important policies below. Share your information with the other participants in the FTA training course.

2. What types of questions are used on tests in the course that you will teach?

3. Are there any traditions concerning tests in the institution in which you are now studying or in the department in which you are teaching? What are they?

9.2 Grading

9.2.a General Information on Grading

Grading is an important factor in a student's life at a college or university. As a grader, you are expected to play judge and jury at times, and this is a difficult task. Keep in mind, however, that grading is a vital function that must be performed in order to evaluate the student's progress in any discipline. There may be times when you will wish that this burden could be assigned to someone else, but you should try to keep in mind that you are performing a necessary task in the educational system. Take grading seriously; if you approach grading with a fair and open mind, it will prove to be less of a burden to you.

If you are required to grade homework problems, quizzes, or tests, there are some important guidelines you should keep in mind.

Check with your department or course coordinator to determine what policies may be in effect. For example, in some departments, it is the policy that the grading method will be to count only correct answers and ignore everything else about the way the student worked the problem. In others, students are given credit for whatever part of a problem they worked correctly (this is called *partial credit*). You must be sure that you follow the department or course policies, if there are any.

Be consistent in your grading practices. Adopt one set of criteria for all the problems or items in each homework set or test, and use them for all the papers you grade in that set. Grade all the students' papers the same way; in other words, be as objective and fair as possible and do not play favorites.

Before the exam or quiz, tell the students what the criteria for grading are, so they will know what to expect. If you are not teaching the course, ask the instructor to tell you what he/she has told the students about grading policy.

If a student asks you to change a grade, take a few days to consider the matter. **Never change a grade on the spot!** Change a grade after a period of time **only** if you made a mistake in the original grading. If you once begin changing grades, you may find many students coming to you for changes in grades (see 3.2.b).

Avoid the problem of having to consider grade changes by grading carefully and completely the first time. Set your grading criteria and follow them. Check periodically to see that you are applying the same criteria to each paper. Also check your work, including addition and averaging of points, for careless errors. Finding a mistake in the addition of the points signals to the student that you have not taken the evaluation of his/her work seriously and may make the student suspect that you have not given careful attention to the paper. The student may then feel free to challenge your grades.

Be reasonable in your evaluation of all answers to questions, but do not be too lenient about it. If you know that the students have been forewarned about what to study and what is expected of them, you should stand firm if a completely incorrect answer is given. Do not be afraid to give failing grades when they are deserved.

If a student is truly unhappy about a grade, take the time to go over the questions with him/her. Show the student exactly where and how he/she failed in the answers. This is not a time for negotiating the grade; this is a time to explain to the student what was incorrect or missing from the answer(s).

If it is not within your power to change a grade, tell the student you will consult with the supervisor or chair and that the student can possibly have a session with the supervisor or chair about the grade. But before you make such an offer to the student, be sure that you have cleared the idea with the supervisor or chair.

Do not let the student dictate your course of action to you. Students have rights—to know how the grading was done, to be assured that the grading was done fairly, to ask to have these matters explained to them. But you, as the grader, have rights as well. Do not be intimidated by threats from the students. If you have done your job correctly, your supervisor or chair should support you in the matter.

BE FAIR BUT FIRM IN ALL YOUR GRADING PRACTICES

9. 2. b Answer-Only Method vs. Partial-Credit Method

In grading tests that contain problems, there are two methods the grader can choose from. Sometimes the choice is determined by the policies of the institution, the department, or the course. It is important for the grader to determine before beginning to grade which method will be used. (It is also important for the students to know before taking the test which method will be used.)

The *answer-only* method gives credit only for the correct answer. In this method, the grader needs to look only at the answer. In fact, if this method is used, the test may be constructed in such a manner that the student is not even required to show how he/she arrived at the answer. For example, the problem may be given, followed by a choice of answers; the student is directed to indicate the correct answer by putting the letter or number in front of it in the appropriate place. In the *answer-only* method, the answer is considered either correct or incorrect; and the student is awarded the prescribed number of points or given a zero for the problem.

The *partial-credit* method is designed to give students points for whatever part of the solution or answer they get correct. For example, a certain number of points may be given for using the correct formula and another number of points given for solving the problem correctly using that formula. Certain mistakes—for example, in calculating the answer or in use of terms—will be penalized by deducting a certain number of points.

A grader who uses the *partial-credit* method needs to make two types of decisions: how many points will be given for setting up a problem correctly and how many for solving the problem or completing the answer; and how many points to deduct for what types of errors. In grading according to the *partial-credit* method, it is extremely important for the grader to be consistent; that is, a given mistake or type of mistake must always be penalized by the same number of points. Some graders find it helpful to keep a list of errors made and the number of points to be deducted, so that when the same error appears on another student's paper the grader will remember the penalty for that error. Also, having such a list will be helpful in explaining to students who might question grades how the grade was determined. (See 3.2.b, 16.6, and 16.7 for more information on effective grading.)

A grader must know the policies of the department for the specific course before determining which grading method to use.

9.3 Record Keeping

It is imperative that you keep complete and accurate records of student attendance and performance. Keeping such records will not only make your job of reporting easier; it will also make it easier for you to answer any questions students may have about the evaluation of their performance.

Attendance records may be required. For some courses, attendance may be a requirement of the course. In such situations, you must know and keep a record of exactly when each student was present. Some teachers call the roll (the names of students in the course) at the beginning of each session. Others have seating charts and take attendance by making a record of students not in their assigned seats at the beginning of the class period. Still others use a sign-in sheet, requiring students to sign their names or to place their initials next to their names on a prepared sheet.

Records of homework attempted and/or problems/questions answered correctly are often kept by the teacher. In the first instance, a record is kept of the fact that the students did all the assigned problems or questions, but no record is kept of which ones were done correctly. The underlying assumption is that the homework is designed to get students to attempt to apply the principles of the course and that the attempt itself is important, whether the students were successful or not. In the second case, records show how successful the students were in their attempts. In some cases, students may receive a part of the course grade based on their rate of success (a percentage, for example, of the possible correct answers). Such records are useful for the teacher in working with students individually to indicate why the students may be having difficulty with certain concepts; for example, if a student did not do the assigned homework or did it incorrectly, then the teacher can indicate to the student which concepts or material need to be worked on.

Records of grades are especially important. As explained in 3.2.b, American students expect to be able to question their grades if they disagree with them. If the teacher does not have complete or accurate records of the grades the students earned on assignments (homework, quizzes, lab reports, or tests), students will be more apt to dispute grades than if complete and accurate records are available.

Whatever types of records are kept, students should be made aware of what they are. For example, if attendance records are kept with a penalty for absences, students need to be informed. If homework records indicate only that the student attempted all the problems or questions, the teacher should let students know that this is the policy.

It is a good idea to have a policy sheet to give to students at the beginning of the course. That sheet should include policies about everything that will be recorded: attendance, homework, penalties for late work, assignments to be graded or only checked for completion, and so on. Whatever policies are indicated on the course syllabus, it will be expected that the teacher will keep the records necessary for enforcing those policies.

In preparing such a policy sheet, it is important to check with the department and/or the course or lab coordinator to be sure that the policies stated are in agreement with the policies of the department for the course. (See 5.2 for more details on preparing a course syllabus.)

PART·THREE
HEARING AND PRONOUNCING AMERICAN ENGLISH

Chapter ♦ 10

Getting Started

♦ OVERVIEW

Your ability to hear and pronounce American English will be a critical determinant of your success as a teaching assistant. Clear, understandable pronunciation is necessary for your students to understand you in class lectures and in interactions with students during class discussions and after class, for example, during office hours.

This section will help you and your instructor to make an initial analysis of your pronunciation and to develop some general strategies for improving your ability to speak and to hear American English.

English is an international language with many national and local dialects (e.g., the English of England, the U.S., India, Australia, and more). In this manual, all uses of the word *English* actually refer to *American English*. The authors greatly respect the validity and status of all varieties of English; however, we recommend that speakers of other varieties adjust their pronunciation so that they will be understood by their American undergraduate students. This pronunciation is, thus, adopted as a communication tool for special, limited use while in the U.S.

◆ PRONUNCIATION

10.1 Analysis

Complete the following sentences. Record your answers using a cassette recorder. When you are finished, please turn off the machine and write your name and the date on the cassette tape before returning it to your teacher, who will then analyze your pronunciation and record that analysis on the tape following your recording.

My name is. . . .

My age is. . . .

I was born in. . . . (Name of city and country)

I grew up in. . . . (Name of city and country)

My native language is. . . .

The other languages that I know are. . . .

Besides the U.S., other countries that I have visited or lived in are. . . .

I graduated from high school in. . . . (What year?)

My education beyond high school is. . . .

The major subject that I studied at school is. . . .

My job is. . . .

I started learning English in. . . . (What year?)

Before coming here, I studied English. . . . (How long? Where?)

The main way that I practice my spoken English now is. . . .

My purpose in studying English now is. . . .

My biggest problem with English is. . . .

Describe your specialized field of study in three or more sentences.

◆ TIPS FOR IMPROVING PRONUNCIATION AND LISTENING ABILITY

10.2 Actively Attend to Pronunciation

Use key words as anchor points in pronouncing as well as in comprehending English.
- The key words receive the main stresses and are loudest, longest, and highest in pitch.
- The pronunciation of non-key words is not very important for comprehension or comprehensibility.

Notice the rhythm and the intonation of language and how they affect meaning.
- Remember the circumstances of situations in which intonation is unusually low or high, or in which the rhythm changes.
- Notice the changes in pronunciation of individual sounds that occur under conditions of unusually slow or unusually rapid tempo.

Pay attention to details in the pronunciation of individual sounds.
- Notice how the pronunciation of sounds changes in context.
- Make a mental note of all new pronunciations you hear.

10.3 Adapt to the American Way of Speaking

Imitate.
- Find an American whom you admire and try to imitate that person's style of speaking and gesturing.
- Play at being an American when you speak.
- Imitate the voices of speakers that you hear on the radio or television.

Use your eyes.
- Pay attention to the lips and facial movements of Americans when they speak.
- Observe your own lips and facial movements by practicing your English in front of a mirror.
- Notice the gestures that accompany speech.

Work to change your pronunciation habits.
- Consciously try to improve your pronunciation.
- Try new patterns of rhythm and intonation in your speech.
- Refine your pronunciation based on your perceptions of American speech and of the pronunciation patterns of those around you.

10.4 Know Yourself

Know your own problems and limitations.
- Be aware of areas in your pronunciation that make it hard for Americans to understand you.
- Work on the areas that are the biggest problems for you.
- Understand the ways in which your native language differs from English.
- Focus on the small as well as the large differences in pronunciation between your native language and English.
- Try to learn English as a new system of pronunciation, instead of relying on your native-language pronunciation when speaking or hearing English.

10.5 Learn Ways to Compensate for Pronunciation Problems

Use intonation, rhythm, voice quality, and gestures to help keep the attention of the audience and to help get your message across.
- Compensate for poor pronunciation by practicing the articulation of key words in your field and by speaking slowly and emphatically, especially when delivering a lecture.
- Reinforce your spoken language through written language, for example, by using the chalkboard, typed handouts, or overhead transparencies.

◆ DELIVERY

10.6 Tips for Improving Delivery

Good speakers pay attention to their audience. When you teach, remember that you are speaking to a particular group of people, not just giving a lecture. This means that you should try to customize the lecture to that particular audience, adapting it so that it will be especially interesting, relevant, and understandable to them. Paying attention to the audience also means keeping your eyes on them as much as possible, moving your gaze around the room to focus on different individuals throughout the lecture. This will help you not only to recognize signs of agreement, attentiveness, and understanding—or their opposites—on the faces of your students, but will also help to maintain eye contact, which is desirable in all kinds of interactions with Americans.

Assignment

1. In a small group, brainstorm ways in which you might customize a presentation in your field to an American student audience. List your ideas here.

_____
_____
_____
_____

2. List the visible signs that you would expect from students to indicate:

Agreement

_____
_____
_____
_____

Attention

_____
_____
_____
_____

Understanding

_____
_____
_____
_____

Lack of agreement

_____
_____
_____
_____

Lack of attention

_____
_____
_____
_____

Lack of understanding

_____
_____
_____
_____

3. When reading aloud from a book, a chart, or an overhead projection, it is essential to maintain eye contact as much as possible. What are some ways that you can maintain a good deal of eye contact while reading aloud?

_____
_____
_____
_____

Good speakers use dramatic and emphatic elements to make presentations more dynamic and interesting. Drama and emphasis make a speaker's message clear and memorable. Drama and emphasis can be added nonverbally through changes in facial expressions, hand or arm gestures, and body orientation or movements. These elements can be signaled verbally through decreased rate, increased loudness, and frequent and substantial changes in pitch. When speaking before an audience, native speakers are apt to use a more careful and exaggerated form of pronunciation than in casual conversation, forcefully articulating every word and avoiding contractions and other types of reductions of words. It is especially important for those who are delivering a speech in a language other than their own native language to make use of these devices for increasing force and clarity in messages.

Assignment

Select a one-paragraph passage from a reading in your field and practice delivering that passage as a speech in front of a mirror several times. The first time, pay special attention to the nonverbal elements mentioned above. The second time, work on speech rate, loudness, and pitch of the voice. The third time you deliver the speech, concentrate on careful and forceful articulation of individual sounds. Finally, practice the speech using a combination of all of these dramatic/emphatic elements.

Chapter ◆ 11

English Vowels and Consonants

◆ OVERVIEW

Each language has a unique inventory of vowel and consonant sounds that occur in combinations to make the syllables and words of the language. For any two languages that you choose, the specific sounds and the allowable combinations that occur will never be exactly the same. In fact, even close dialects of the same language differ in the pronunciation of certain vowels and consonants in context.

Attention to the exact features of the pronunciation of individual sounds in American English and how these differ from your native language sounds will put you in a better position to understand and pronounce American English well. This chapter will help you to focus on the obvious and not-so-obvious distinctions in the pronunciation of sounds in American English as compared with other languages.

11.1 Noticing Lip Shapes

In speaking English, the lips are constantly in motion. For some sounds, the lips are spread. For others, they are rounded. For still others, they are neutral, that is, neither spread nor rounded. In English, the lip shape of a sound is often anticipated by another sound that comes earlier in the same word. For example, in the word *tea*, the /t/ is pronounced with spread lips in anticipation of the following vowel, while in the word *too*, the /t/ is pronounced with rounded lips. When pronouncing or hearing English, learn to be aware of the visible movements of the lips.

Assignment

Group the underlined English sounds below into the three columns shown in the table.

r<u>e</u>d	moth<u>er</u>	<u>s</u>et	<u>v</u>an
<u>ea</u>t	b<u>u</u>t	<u>sh</u>oe	<u>l</u>ean
w<u>e</u>nt	s<u>o</u>	l<u>i</u>p	l<u>oo</u>p
dem<u>o</u>cratic	ma<u>ch</u>ine	s<u>oo</u>n	b<u>oo</u>k
s<u>o</u>n	h<u>o</u>t	b<u>a</u>d	<u>e</u>thic

Stretched Lips	Rounded Lips	Neutral Lips

11.2 Pronunciation Modeling

In speaking English, the lips are in constant motion. Moving the lips in certain ways is part of the pronunciation of English sounds. In many cases, the lip movements are more dramatic than those used in the pronunciation of the sounds of other languages.

Assignment

1. Pronounce each of the words below slowly and carefully. Pay attention to how your lips and tongue move in the pronunciation of each. Then watch another student pronounce the words.

pew	bugle	cube	few	hue
pure	beauty	accuse	fury	huge
dispute	abuse	argue	refuse	human
sphere	skew	splat	sclerosis	
sphinx	spew	squat	thwart	

2. Pick out ten key words of one, two, or three syllables from your field of specialization. These should be words that occur frequently in your field or the textbook you will use in your class. Now "dictate" these words silently to a partner, that is, mouth the pronunciation of the words by moving only your lips. First, say aloud the number of the word you will "dictate." Then mouth the word silently three times before going on to the next word. Then reverse roles with your partner.

Discuss any difficulties that you had with each other's words.

11.3 Comparison of English to Native-Language Vowels

Below are shown the vowel sounds of English. Notice that the English vowel sounds do not correspond one-to-one with the vowel spellings. Compare these with the vowel sounds in your language. How many different vowel sounds do you think there are in your language?

Assignment

Place each one of the vowel sounds in your language in one of the three categories in the table below, depending on whether it is exactly the same as an English vowel sound, a little bit different, or completely different.

English Vowel Sounds

(1)	heat	/iy/				(8)	hoot	/uw/
(2)	hit	/ɪ/				(9)	hook	/u/
(3)	hate	/ey/				(10)	hoed	/ow/
(4)	head	/ɛ/	(7)	hut	/ə/	(11)	hawk	/ɔ/
(5)	hat	/æ/	(6)	hot	/a/			
(12)	hide	/ay/	(13)	how	/aw/	(14)	hoist	/ɔy/

Exactly the Same	A Little Bit Different	Completely Different

11.4 Special Features of English Vowels

English has more vowel sounds than are found in many other languages. Therefore, many speakers will have to learn to make new distinctions in pronunciation that are not necessary in the native language. For all speakers, it will be necessary to learn a new vowel system, though some parts of the system may closely resemble that of the native language.

English has four distinct sets of vowels:

Spread (Front):	/iy/, /ɪ/, /ey/, /ɛ/, /æ/
Neutral (Central):	/ə/, /a/
Rounded (Back):	/uw/, /ʊ/, /ow/, /ɔ/
Combinations:	/ay/ (Neutral-Spread), /aw/ (Neutral-Rounded or Spread-Rounded, depending on dialect), /ɔy/ (Rounded-Spread)

As compared with other languages, English vowel sounds tend to be relatively long and nonhomogeneous. This means that the quality of an English vowel tends not to be "pure" but rather to change somewhat during the course of pronouncing it. In most cases, active shaping and movement of the lips will be required for nativelike English pronunciation. For the three vowel combinations, an extreme degree of lip shaping and movement is necessary for good pronunciation.

English has vowel pairs where many languages have only one vowel. In these cases, it is necessary to learn to distinguish carefully the two English sounds, which may overlap one native language sound, in both production and perception. The following are the pairs of sounds that might be confused because both of them overlap with one sound in many other languages:

/iy/ vs. /ɪ/

/ey/ vs. /ɛ/

The first member in each of these oppositions is significantly longer, tenser (i.e., it requires more effort and muscular tension), more spread, and less pure than the second. Moreover, the second sound in each pair requires opening the jaw (i.e., the mouth in a vertical direction) more than the first sound.

/uw/ vs. /ʊ/

/ow/ vs. /ɔ/

The difference between these pairs is similar to that of the front pairs except that, in this case, the first member of each opposition is more rounded than the latter. Otherwise, the same description applies here as applies to that for the front vowel pairs; that is, the first member of the pair is longer, tenser, and less pure than the second, and the second member of the pair has greater vertical jaw opening than the first.

/æ/ vs. /a/

Both of these vowels have the mouth widely open in a vertical direction. However, only the first requires spreading the lips at the same time that the jaw is near its maximal opening. We can say that /æ/ is both a "vertical" and a "horizontal" sound, whereas /a/ is "vertical" only.

/ə/

The sound represented by /ə/ in the chart, the sound called *schwa*, is the most common vowel sound by far in the English language. This is so because under conditions of weak stress, which is very common in fluent English speech, all vowels tend to lose their distinctive pronunciation. Under these conditions, all vowels tend to become "neutralized," that is, they end up being pronounced as the one vowel that has the mouth neither very open nor very closed, and the lips neither spread nor rounded. This is the schwa vowel.

11.5 Comparison of English to Native-Language Consonants

ENGLISH CONSONANT SOUNDS

	Stop Sounds		Continuant Sounds		Nasal Sounds
	Voiced	*Voiceless*	*Voiced*	*Voiceless*	*Voiced*
Two Lips	b	p	w	(wh)	m
Teeth + Lip			v	f	
Teeth + Tongue			ð	θ	
Tongue Tip	d	t	z, l, r	s	n
Tongue Front			ž, y, j	š, č	
Tongue Back	g	k			ŋ
Throat				h	

Key to Symbols

b	*b*e	k	*k*iss	l	*l*ip	wh	*wh*ite	č	*ch*in
d	*d*o	w	*w*e	r	*r*un	f	*f*ill	h	*h*ot
g	*g*o	v	*v*an	ž	vi*si*on	θ	*th*in	m	*m*an
p	*p*oor	ð	*th*en	y	*y*es	s	*s*o	n	*n*o
t	*t*o	z	*z*ip	j	*j*udge	š	*sh*ow	ŋ	so*ng*

Assignment

Compare the consonant sounds of your native language with those of English. Put each of the consonant sounds of your language under one of the headings in the table below, depending on whether it is exactly the same, a little bit different, or completely different as compared with an English consonant sound.

Exactly the Same	**A Little Bit Different**	**Completely Different**

11.6 Special Features of English Consonants

As in all languages, English makes a distinction between voiced and voiceless sounds. Voiced sounds are produced with vibration of the vocal cords; you can feel this vibration by holding your index finger on your Adam's apple or covering your ears with the palms of your hands while pronouncing a sustained /a/. Voiceless sounds are produced with no vocal cord vibration. They are essentially made only by pushing air out of the lungs and then out through the mouth.

English has three basic consonant series:

Stop sounds

These are produced with a complete closure at the two lips (/p, b/), at the tongue tip and the gum ridge (/t, d/), or at the tongue back and the back of the roof of the mouth (/k, g/). The stop sounds /p, t, k/ are distinguished from /b, d, g/ in that they have a longer period of closure and, when they occur at the beginning of an accented word or syllable, are aspirated, that is, produced with a puff of air. The English initials /p, t, k/ are relatively breathy as compared with the same sounds in many other languages. In unaccented internal or final positions, the stop sounds /p, t, k/ are usually pronounced without the puff of air.

Continuant sounds

These are produced without a complete closure anywhere in the vocal tract. This means that the sounds can continue for as long as the speaker forms the sound and has breath remaining to continue pronouncing. All vowels are continuant sounds, and the largest of the three classes of consonants in English are also continuant sounds. Sometimes the native language will not make the same distinctions between stops and continuants as are made in English, so that the following sounds may be confused: /p, f, wh/, /b, v, w/, /t, θ, s/, /d, ð, z/. In each of these groups, only the first sound is a stop sound, whereas the other two are continuants.

Nasal sounds

English has three sounds produced by having air escape through the nose. One of these is pronounced with the two lips together (/m/), one with the tongue tip against the gum ridge (/n/), and one with the tongue back against the back of the roof of the mouth (/ŋ/).

The difference between some pairs of consonant sounds is partially in a tendency for the lips to be either spread or rounded. In the following pairs, the first sound tends to have spread lips and the second, rounded lips: /v, w/, /z, ž/, /s, š/, /l, r/.

Watch English speakers when they pronounce these sounds, and practice making the distinction between spread and rounded lips to make your own pronunciation easier for Americans to understand.

Some pairs of sounds can be distinguished in that one is a homogeneous continuant sound, whereas the other is made up of a combination of a stop sound plus a following continuant sound. Such pairs are the following: /š, č/, /ž, ǰ/

/š/ (continuant)   /č/ (stop /t/ + continuant /š/)

/ž/ (continuant)   /ǰ/ (stop /d/ + continuant /ž/)

In order to produce a clear /ð/ or /θ/, it is essential to extend the tongue between the teeth so that the tip is clearly visible. If the tongue touches the teeth but does not extend between the teeth, the sound produced will resemble /t/ or /d/ more than /θ/ or /ð/. If the tongue tip is not quite touching the teeth and is pointing up toward the gum ridge, the sound produced will resemble /s/ or /z/ more than /θ/ or /ð/.

Notice that there are seven English sounds produced with the tongue tip. Unlike similar sounds in many other languages, for the English sounds, the tongue does not quite touch the teeth. Rather, the tip of the tongue is at the gum ridge just behind the top teeth.

11.7 Consonant Combinations, Section 1

English has many combinations of two or more consonants. The pronunciation of such combinations of consonants is often difficult for non-native speakers, who may tend to separate the two consonants for ease of pronunciation by placing a weak vowel in between. The exercise below should help you in articulating these consonant combinations and in avoiding the production of a weak vowel between the two consonants.

It is important to articulate Consonant + Consonant combinations clearly and distinctly and yet still to differentiate them from similar-sounding syllables of the type Consonant + Weak Vowel + Consonant. As a first kind of practice, try to distinguish between the words on the left and the words on the right in the vocabulary lists that follow by pronouncing the words according to the intonation lines. (The meaning of words that you might not know is given in parentheses, since it is hard to learn to pronounce unknown words.) You will notice that the one-syllable words represented by the left-hand list begin with a relatively high pitch, which falls throughout the pronunciation of the word. In the two-syllable words represented by the right-hand list, the pitch begins low and then steps up all at once, rather than rising gradually.

Vocabulary

train	terrain	(territory, piece of earth)
drive	derive	(obtain, deduce, infer)
prayed	parade	

Assignment

Discrimination Practice
　　Each of the sentences below contains a blank space that can be filled by either of the two words following. Your teacher or another student will say the sentence using one of the two words to the right to fill in the blank space. Listen to his/her pronunciation to try to decide which word was selected. To decide, pay attention to the intonation.

1. The _____ here is excellent.　　train　　terrain
2. How did you _____ that?　　drive　　derive
3. The word is _____ .　　prayed　　parade

　　Notice that all of the two-syllable words (all those in the second column) have a very weak first vowel and a dramatic contrast in stress between the first and second syllable.

11.8 Consonant Combinations, Section 2

Practice making a sharp distinction between the one-syllable words on the left, all of which begin with a consonant cluster, and the two-syllable words on the right, all of which have a weak first syllable. Remember:

For the One-Syllable Words
a. The pitch falls gradually.
b. There is no vowel sound between the consonants.

For the Two-Syllable Words
a. The pitch steps up to the second syllable.
b. The vowel of the first syllable is weakened to schwa, and the second syllable is forcefully pronounced.

One Syllable

train

drive

prayed

bray (make a donkey sound)

crowed (made a rooster sound)

plight (desperate situation)

blow

claps

flay (cut the skin off)

Two Syllables

terrain (territory, piece of earth)

derive (obtain, deduce, infer)

parade

beret

corrode (wear away gradually)

polite

below

collapse

filet (cut into boneless pieces)

Assignment

1. Practice the following sentences.

    The rocky *terrain* of Utah is breathtakingly beautiful.
    How did you *derive* that result?
    The little boy *prayed* that it would not rain on the *parade*.

2. Work with a partner to practice some of the words in the following sentences. Choose one of the words to the right of each sentence. Then say the sentence, putting the word you selected in the blank space. If your pronunciation is correct, your partner should be able to guess which word you have said. Alternate turns with your partner and keep practicing until each of you is pronouncing and hearing the words correctly every time.

   1. This _____ makes for a rough ride.   train   terrain
   2. Can you show me how to _____ it?   drive   derive
   3. I would like you to _____ the fish.   flay   filet

3. Find at least five important words from your field that contain a combination of two or more consonants and are difficult for you to pronounce. Make a tape recording of your voice, using each of the words you have chosen in a sentence that represents a typical context for the word in your field. Bring your tape to class to receive feedback on your pronunciation.

11.9 Comparing the Pronunciation of Words in English and the Native Language

Much of the technical and scientific vocabulary of the world is derived from the same roots, often originally from Indo-European languages. Though these words may have the same origin in American English and your native language and may even be spelled the same in the two languages, the pronunciation may be quite different. This is because each language adopts new words from other languages by modifying their pronunciation to fit the conventions of the receiving language.

Assignment

1. Do you have any of the following words in your native language? If so, compare the pronunciation of the word in your language with that of your classmates from other countries and with American English. Such a comparison can help you to focus on the ways in which your native pronunciation differs from that of other languages, especially American English.

   machine

   equipment

   technique

   computer

   automobile

   oscilloscope

   calculator

2. Practice pronouncing these words with a partner in the American English way.

3. Find ten specialized words from your field that have English equivalents, and practice making the contrast between your native pronunciation and the American English pronunciation. Record both pronunciations on tape so that you can receive feedback on your pronunciation.

Chapter ♦ 12

Stress Patterns in English Words and Sentences

♦ OVERVIEW

One of the most important distinguishing features of fluent English speech is the pattern of strong and weak stresses, or accents, that occur in words and sentences. By attending to the strong stresses within the stream of speech, we can often recognize key words in a message and comprehend the general meaning of a discourse, even if the details are not comprehensible. Conversely, placing the stresses in a spoken discourse incorrectly or pronouncing certain words or syllables too strongly or too weakly makes it very difficult for a listener to understand spoken language. Mastery of the stress and rhythmic patterns of English therefore gives the non-native speaker a head start in both listening comprehension and pronunciation.

This chapter addresses this important aspect of language at both the word and sentence level.

12.1 English Syllables and Stress

English words and sentences are made up of an alternating pattern of strong and weak syllables. This alternating pattern of strong and weak syllables comprises the rhythm of the language. Every language has a different rhythmic pattern; and natural-sounding pronunciation, as well as full comprehension, can be achieved only when this rhythmic pattern is mastered.

As a general rule, every English word spoken in isolation contains one major syllable. This major syllable is said to be stressed. In English, a stressed, or strong, syllable is usually louder, and its vowel is longer and higher pitched than the vowel of an unstressed, or weak, syllable. Often, the vowel of an unstressed syllable is shortened or weakened to the neutral *schwa* vowel. Typically, it is only in strong, stressed syllables that vowels are pronounced in their full form.

Each of the words below has a weak (unaccented) first syllable and a strong (accented) second syllable. An accented syllable is generally longer, louder, and higher in pitch than an unaccented syllable. An accent mark indicates the beginning of the stressed syllable. A line drawn through the vowel of the first syllable indicates that this vowel is only minimally pronounced. Practice the pronunciation of these words, making the vowel of the first syllable as minimal as you can and emphasizing the second syllable.

cøn 'vert   prø 'duce   dı̸ 'rect   prø 'mote   ad 'vise   prɇ 'dict

Assignment

In the examples below, the beginning of the strong syllable is indicated by an accent mark, and a slash mark is drawn through weak vowels. The pitch pattern (intonation) is represented by a continuous line. [Note: The *ti* in the ending *-tion* is pronounced /š/.]

Practice the pronunciation of these words with a partner.

'in sult   ın 'sult   ın 'sul tɇd

                 ap 'ply   ap 'ply ıng   ap plı̸ 'ca tiøn

'port   'por tage   dɇ 'port   dɇ 'port mɇnt   de pør 'ta tiøn

'solve   'sol vɇnt   rɇ 'solve   rɇ 'sol vıng   re sø 'lu tiøn

12.2 Identifying Strong and Weak Stresses

In many words, such as *prø 'duc tiøn* and *cøn 'ver siøn*, there are two or more weak syllables together with one strong syllable.

Assignment

1. In the list below, circle the words that have the same pattern of strong and weak syllables as *production* and *conversion*. Mark the weak syllables by slashes through the vowels and the strong syllables with accent marks. Practice the pronunciation of these words.

   financial   advancement   storage   potential

   sequence   apply   director   placement

2. In the following words, the final syllable *-tion* is weak, pronounced /šən/. Which other syllable is quite weak in these words? Mark this syllable in each word with a slash and practice pronouncing the vowel minimally.

dis tri ′bu tiøn   i so ′la tiøn

com pu ′ta tiøn   ap pli ′ca tiøn

com pe ′ti tiøn

Notice that in each of these four-syllable words, there is a weak syllable right before the strong, or accented, syllable. It is typical in English for a strong syllable—whether in a word or a sentence—to be preceded by one or more weak syllables. The strong syllable is highlighted by the contrast with a preceding context of weak syllables.

Also notice that it does not matter what the spelling of the vowel is in an unaccented (unstressed) syllable; the weak pronunciation is virtually always the same schwa sound.

12.3 Noun and Verb Pairs With Different Stress

There are a number of words in English that are derived from the same root and that are spelled the same way but that are either nouns or verbs, depending on the stress pattern. In these words, the vowel of the unstressed syllable is weakened to schwa, and there is an intonational step—either up or down—between the first and the second syllable.

Assignment

For the two lists below, label one "nouns" and the other "verbs." Then draw in the proper pitch patterns and draw a line through the reduced vowel in each word. Afterwards, practice the pronunciation of these words in appropriate academic contexts on tape or with a partner.

record	record
subject	subject
object	object
suspect	suspect
present	present
insult	insult

12.4 Strongly Stressed Vowels, Section 1

Vowels in English vary in pronunciation depending on context. In one-syllable words out of context, the vowel is generally strongly pronounced. In the context of a word of more than one syllable, a vowel may be pronounced strongly or weakly, depending on whether it is stressed. It is important to know how to pronounce the vowels in long and short words according to the stress pattern.

Assignment

1. Practice the pronunciation of the following English vowel sounds:
    /iy/ as in *heat*
    /ɪ/ as in *hit*
    /ey/ as in *hate*
    /ɛ/ as in *head*
    /æ/ as in *hat*

2. Working with a partner or a dictionary, group the words below into five lists so that each list contains four words whose strongest stressed vowel is the same as the vowel shown at the top of that list.

evasive	regal	prophetic	sagacious	unsettling
appease	cyclic	saturnine	embattled	citric
educated	archaic	appetite	metric	grievous
situated	endangered	regional	rhythmic	apparatus

List 1 /iy/	List 2 /ɪ/	List 3 /ey/	List 4 /ɛ/	List 5 /æ/

3. Now, add four additional words of two or more syllables to each list. Then pick three words from each list and make a tape recording of your pronunciation of these words in a sentence typical for your field of study. Bring the tape recording in to class so that you can receive feedback on your pronunciation.

12. 5 Strongly Stressed Vowels, Section 2

Pronouncing a word so that the proper vowel receives the strongest stress is an essential part of intelligible English pronunciation.

Assignment

1. Practice the pronunciation of the following English vowel sounds:

/ə/ as in *hut*
/uw/ as in *hoot*
/ʊ/ as in *hook*
/ow/ as in *hoed*
/ɔ/ as in *hawk*

Chapter 12 Stress Patterns in English Words and Sentences

2. Working with a partner or a dictionary, group the words below into five lists so that each list contains four words whose strongest stressed vowel is the same as the vowel shown at the top of that list.

associate	superman	government	fuller	constructive
understood	luster	supper	movable	awesome
remote	oddness	rudeness	unsuitable	unhook
exhaust	disposal	thoughtful	owner	mistook

List 1 /ə/	List 2 /uw/	List 3 /ʊ/	List 4 /ow/	List 5 /ɔ/

3. Now, add four additional words of two or more syllables to each list. Then pick three words from each list and make a tape recording of your pronunciation of these words in a sentence typical of your field of study. Bring the tape recording in to class so that you can receive feedback on your pronunciation.

12.6 Stress Patterns in Academic Words

In English words of three or more syllables, the stress patterns are highly variable, though there are some regularities.

Assignment

1. Group the following words into five lists of words, with the same pattern of strong and weak syllables in each list. Use the key word of each list as a guide in finding other words of the same pattern. Mark the strong and weak syllables and practice the pronunciation of the words. Remember that the weak syllables are those pronounced with a schwa /ə/. [Note: the *ti* in the ending *-tion* is pronounced /š/.]

List 1	List 2	List 3	List 4	List 5
(6 words)	(3 words)	(5 words)	(3 words)	(2 words)
pre ′dic tion	′tech ni cal	com ′pe ti tor	ma ni pu ′la tion	i so ′la tion

promotional	component	conversion
advisory	production	manufacture
examine	management	manipulate
determination	classification	sequential
capable	effectively	

2. Find ten key words from your field that are difficult for you to pronounce and that contain at least three syllables. Locate the weak and strong syllables and the reduced vowels in the words and mark these. Then practice the pronunciation of the words with a partner.

12.7 Matching Words to Stress Patterns

For much of the academic vocabulary of English, a certain root (often derived from Latin) is the basis for a large group of related words. In the left-hand column of the list on page 102 are five common roots from which a number of English words are derived. The different words derived from each root have different patterns of strong and weak stresses.

Assignment

Working with another class member or with a dictionary, find words formed from each root to match the stress patterns shown. For each word, the number of syllables in the word is shown by the number of blank spaces. The syllable that receives the strongest stress is marked by /′/ at the beginning of the syllable.

Chapter 12 *Stress Patterns in English Words and Sentences*

1. TECH   ex.   a. ′<u>tech</u> <u>ni</u> <u>cal</u>   b. ___ ′___
          c. ___ ___ ′___ ___

2. AUD   a. ___ ′___ ___   b. ′___ ___ ___ ___
          c. ___ ___ ′___ ___

3. CLASS   a. ′___ ___ ___   b. ′___ ___ ___ ___
          c. ___ ___ ___ ′___

4. ATOM   a. ′___ ___ ___   b. ___ ′___ ___
          c. ___ ___ ___ ′___

5. SYSTEM a. ___ ___ ′___ ___   b. ′___ ___ ___ ___
          c. ___ ___ ___ ___ ′___ ___

12.8 More Practice in Pronouncing Longer Words

The words below are commonly occurring words in an academic context that non-native speakers may accent incorrectly. They are grouped according to the syllable that receives the strongest stress. These are all important words, which you should practice pronouncing until you are confident that a native speaker would not misunderstand you.

You may wish to add other words that you need to practice to these lists.

Stress on First Syllable	Stress on Second Syllable	Stress on Third Syllable
inference	assignment	information
exercises	discussion	education
necessary	activity	introduction
concentrate	conclusion	university
management	impossible	satisfactory
library	experience	academic
reference	prediction	hypothetical
controversy	material	controversial

12.9 Stress in Context, Section 1

When words occur in the context of phrases or sentences, their stress is adjusted somewhat to conform to the rhythmic patterns of longer utterances. In general, the important words (nouns, verbs, adjectives, or adverbs) or those containing focused information (information that is newly introduced or that is central to the topic under discussion) receive the strongest stresses. In addition, roots of words tend to be stressed, whereas the endings of words tend to be reduced.

Assignment

1. For each of the words and phrases below, underline the syllable that will receive the strongest stress.

2. Then practice the pronunciation of the words and phrases, making a sharp distinction between the accented and unaccented syllables. Compare your pronunciation with that of your teacher or another student.

Nouns	Verbs	Adjectives
the subject	was subjected to	subjective
the object	is objecting	objectionable
in the application	has been applying	applicable
the management of	has managed to	manageable
the necessity of	necessitated	necessary
as a hypothesis	hypothesizes	hypothetical
in conclusion	to conclude	conclusive
a conversion of	converted	convertible
the production of	will have produced	producible
in our discussion	were discussing	discussable
a controversy	controverted	controversial
as an inference from	inferred	inferential

12.10 Stress in Context, Section 2

It is important for you as a teacher to learn to stress the important words in your lectures to make the content easier for the students to follow.

Assignment

1. Which word or words would you stress in using the following phrases in a lecture? Why? Underline the word you would stress, and then write the reason for stressing it.

To begin with. . . . _____

As I stated yesterday, . . . _____

To begin where we left off yesterday, . . . _____

The point is that. . . . _____

The point is exactly that. _____

Do any of you disagree that. . . . _____

I hope some of you will disagree. _____

In contrast to his position. . . . _____

My position is in contrast to his position. _____

_____

In order for this mechanism to function, . . . _____

_____

In order for this mechanism to function at all, . . . _____

_____

In order for this mechanism to function at all adequately, . . . _____

_____

2. Practice making a sharp contrast between the strongly stressed and unstressed syllables in these examples.

3. What gestures of the hands or face might accompany each of the preceding phrases?

12.11 Contrastive/Emphatic Stress

A word or phrase that receives strong stress (indicated by a combination of loudness, high pitch, and lengthening of vowel) receives special emphasis or contrast in a sentence.

Assignment

1. Pronounce the following sentences using the different stress patterns indicated, and discuss the difference in meaning associated with each stress pattern.

 ′I think so.

 I ′think so.

 I think ′so.

 Do not touch the chemicals in the ′blue ′jars.

Do not touch the chemicals in the ′blue jars.

′Do ′not ′touch the ′chemicals in the ′blue ′jars!

I disa ′gree.

I ′disagree.

′I disagree.

The statement is absolutely ′false.

The statement is ′absolutely ′false.

The statement ′is absolutely false.

2. If you want feedback on your pronunciation of these sentences, make a tape recording of your pronunciation of each of them, and bring it to class.

Chapter ♦ 13

The Units of Fluent Speech

♦ OVERVIEW

In fluent speech, we show the relationships between ideas by grouping words together into phrases, pausing in appropriate places, and "bridging" to ease pronunciation between sounds. An awareness of these processes of fluent speech will make it easier for you to understand native speakers and also make it easier for them to understand you. This chapter introduces the most important aspects of fluent speech phenomena in English.

13.1 Thought Groups

When speakers organize their ideas into sentences and longer discourses, they need to indicate to the listener the main groupings of ideas. In English, the groupings of ideas, called *thought groups*, are generally indicated in the following ways:

- A thought group is spoken in one breath.
- A thought group does not contain internal pauses but may be surrounded by pauses.
- A thought group has only one highlighted word, that is, only one word that receives a strong stress.

The length of a thought group varies depending on the rate of speech and the emphasis intended by the speaker. The following tendencies have been noted by researchers:

- In rapid speech, thought groups are longer than in slow or emphatic speech.
- The more we want to emphasize the message of our words, the more we use separate thought groups.
- In very emphatic speech, we might make every word in a phrase or sentence a separate thought group.

Assignment

1. In the sentences below, thought groups have been marked by slash marks. Practice the sentences, pausing where the slashes are marked.

   /If I said that,/I was lying./

   /If I said that I was lying,/I was telling the truth./

   /If I said that I was lying in that context,/then I probably was telling the truth./

   /What I said was the truth./That's always the best policy./

   /What I said was:/"The truth:/That's always the best policy."/

   /Be sure to turn in your homework on time./

   /Don't/you/dare/not to turn in/your homework/on time./

   /How did you end up with that answer?/

   /How in the world/did you end up/with that answer?/

   Until you get used to speaking English in front of a group, it might be wise to use relatively short thought groups. If you speak from a prepared text or read passages from a textbook in class, you could mark thought groups in advance and use these markings as a guide while speaking.

2. Mark a short passage from a textbook to indicate thought groups. Then ask another person to look at the passage and your markings. Discuss any suggestions about possible differences in ways to mark thought groups. Decide on a final marking for the passage.

3. Make a tape recording of yourself reading the passage according to the way you have marked it. Listen to it carefully to see if you actually broke the sentences into meaningful groups. Ask your teacher to give you feedback on your reading.

4. Read the passage aloud to the class as though it were part of a class lecture. That is, stand at the front of the class to do the reading. After you look down at the passage to get a phrase in mind, look up at the class to regain eye contact as you say the words. Practice this activity at home. Your purposes are to read well and also to maintain eye contact rather than looking down at the passage the entire time that you are reading.

108 Chapter 13 *The Units of Fluent Speech*

13.2 Bridging

Unlike many other languages that tend to keep individual words separate in continuous speech, English is characterized by a high degree of linking, or *bridging,* between words. Bridging is very common in American speech and so helps to identify a native or nativelike accent. Being able to make these "sound bridges" between words will therefore help to improve your image as a second language speaker and may make it easier for American students to understand you. Moreover, your own listening comprehension can be aided significantly by attending to the bridges that native speakers commonly make between words.

In normal pronunciation the speaker will often form sound bridges from one word to the next in one of the following ways:

1. By continuing a final consonant into the pronunciation of a following word that begins with a vowel.

Phrase	Bridge	Pronounced As
stop it	/p/	/sta pɪt/
give it	/v/	/gɪ vɪt/
one of	/n/	/wə nəv/
his idea	/z/	/hɪ zaydɪə/

2. By dropping an initial /h/ in the second word and then bridging as in 1 above.

where he	/r/	/wɛ riy/
when his	/n/	/wɛ nɪz/
had her	/d/	/hæ dər/
liked him	/t/	/layk tɪm/

3. By adding a gliding sound between a word ending with a vowel and the following word beginning with a vowel.

the idea	/y/	/ði yaydɪə/
the answer	/y/	/ði yænsər/
know it	/w/	/no wɪt/
though it's	/w/	/ðo wɪts/

Assignment

1. Practice bridging between the words in the examples above by working with a native speaker or a classmate.
2. Make a tape recording of yourself while reading a passage aloud from one of your textbooks. Then check to see how many of the potential bridges between words you have realized in your pronunciation.
3. Tape yourself again, first reading the same passage aloud and then reading another passage, paying special attention to the bridging between words.

Chapter ◆ 14

Intonation and Voice Quality

◆ OVERVIEW

By varying intonation, or vocal pitch, and voice quality, speakers signal many different kinds of meaning. Moreover, listeners often respond as much or more to intonation and voice quality as to the content of our words. It is therefore important to be able to make the same variations in intonation and voice quality that native English speakers use and respond to. Equally important is a knowledge of the appropriate circumstances for use of a certain intonation or voice quality. This chapter presents an overview of these important aspects of communication and their functions for English speakers.

14.1 Intonation, Section 1

When speaking any language, a person makes the voice rise and fall in pitch. The patterns of pitches that occur in continuous speech are referred to as *intonation patterns*. Except in cases of special emphasis or contrast, an English clause or sentence has the major pitch change on the last major content word. This is entirely appropriate, considering that it is also a pattern in English for the most important or least predictable (i.e., new) information to be placed at or near the end of a sentence. We can therefore call final position the "focal," or highlighted, position. In this position, the major pitch change of the sentence draws attention to this highlighted information.

In statements or information questions (those beginning with words such as *who, when, why*), the pitch typically rises and then falls on the last major content word or phrase. In yes/no questions, the pitch of the voice tends to be high and/or to rise on the last major content word. In enumeration, the voice is high or rises on all of the items other than the last one, to show that more information is coming. This pattern can be called the "continuation" intonational pattern. Thus we can see that falling intonation generally indicates finality, whereas rising or high intonation generally indicates nonfinality. Examples of each of these patterns are given below. Practice these with a classmate.

Statement/Wh-Question

1. I want you to take out your study sheets now.

2. This chapter is an important one.

3. Where is your study sheet?

4. Who knows the answer to this question?

Yes/No Question

1. Do you know the answer to this question?

2. Have you read the assignment yet?

3. Do you agree with the opinion expressed here?

4. Will you be able to finish your paper on time?

Continuation

1. Either he is lying, or he is misguided.

2. There are four things you need to do by the end of the course:

   turn in your lab reports, turn in your class notes, schedule a meeting with me,

   and then turn in your final papers.

3. The reason could be the obvious one, or it could be a not-so-obvious one.

4. You will either have to take a makeup exam or else retake the course.

14.2 Intonation, Section 2

In some languages—for example, Chinese, Thai, Vietnamese, and many African languages—individual words have characteristic pitch patterns. In such languages, these patterns of pitches, called *tones*, help to differentiate otherwise synonymous words. Besides the patterns of tones in individual words, *tone languages* also have intonation patterns extending over whole sentences. However, the specific intonation pattern is to a large extent determined by the tone patterns of individual words.

In English, intonation patterns are determined more by the meaning of entire sentences and longer discourses than by the specific words that occur in a sentence. In fact, the stress pattern of an individual word can change to accommodate to the more powerful influence of the whole sentence context. For example, the strongest stress (and so the major pitch change) in sentence 1 below is on the last syllable of *seventeen* since this is the most important, that is, the focused, word in the sentence. In sentence 2, in contrast, where the focused word is *dollars*, the stress on the last syllable of *seventeen* is de-emphasized to avoid having two strong stresses in succession. The major pitch on this word shifts to the first syllable under those circumstances.

1. The number is seven ′teen.

2. It costs ′seventeen ′dollars.

In English, intonation is constantly changing, sliding up and down in a sentence or longer discourse.

Assignment

1. Make a recording of a native English speaker from the television or radio and note the use of intonation.

2. Using a second tape recorder, make a recording of your own voice, attempting to imitate the speaker as closely as possible sentence by sentence. Then listen to the original recording and your imitations, stopping after each sentence to analyze the native speaker's and your own performance.

3. Write down ideas for yourself to try to improve your intonation.
_____
_____
_____
_____
_____

14.3 Voice Quality

Each language has a characteristic voice quality that gives its speakers a recognizable accent when speaking another language. This is partly a matter of rhythmic and pitch patterns, but voice quality is also related to the position of the tongue and the shape of the lips when pronouncing individual sounds. Compare your native language with the languages described in terms of parameters of voice quality.

PITCH	Chinese:	Determined at Word and Sentence Level
	English:	Determined at Sentence Level
	Your Native Language:	
STRESS	Spanish:	Relatively Uniform
	English:	Highly Variable
	Your Native Language:	
LIPS	Japanese:	Not Very Active
	English:	Active
	Your Native Language:	
TONGUE TIP	Hindi:	Usually Retroflex (turned up and pointed backward)
	English:	Usually Non-Retroflex
	Your Native Language:	

In addition to the voice qualities that we can identify with different language backgrounds, we can also notice different voice qualities within one language. Some of these differences comprise differences in dialect, whereas others are identified with certain roles or moods of the speaker. For some speakers of English, the main body of the tongue is characteristically retracted, or back, and as a result the tip of the tongue is not very much involved in the articulation of individual sounds. For other speakers, the tongue tip is very active in the pronunciation of sounds such as /s/, /z/, /t/, /d/, /l/, and /n/. Different dialects of English also have characteristic lip shapes.

Assignment

1. Discuss with your teacher and classmates the connotations that you associate with each of the voice qualities listed.
   a. a very high-pitched voice
   b. a very low-pitched voice
   c. a muffled voice quality
   d. very careful articulation
   e. extremely slow speech
   f. very quiet speech
   g. very loud speech

2. Make up a sentence of at least five words to express each of the roles or emotions listed. Use voice quality, body posture, facial expression, and gestures where appropriate to express the role or emotion in each case.
   a. dominance or authority
   b. submission or lack of confidence
   c. extreme sadness or depression
   d. excitement or enthusiasm
   e. hostility or aggression
   f. extreme informality
   g. extreme formality
   h. dislike
   i. friendliness

3. In a group, compare and contrast the qualities you used to produce each of the roles listed above with those used by others in the group.

4. Finally, try expressing these roles using voice qualities that you think are American. If there is disagreement, ask your teacher or another native American English speaker for clarification.

Part ◆ FOUR

PRACTICE FOR TEACHING

Chapter ◆ 15

Learning to Give Short Explanations

◆ OVERVIEW

Teaching undergraduates at a U.S. university involves three main areas: (1) subject-area expertise, (2) speaking skills, and (3) human-relations skills. This book is designed to help foreign teaching assistants improve their competence in the last two of those areas. Part Four focuses on the skills needed for the kinds of speaking done by teachers in classrooms. This speaking can range from very formal speeches on theoretical topics to informal discussions of mathematics problems to presentations of laboratory exercises. In all of these situations, the teacher talks to groups of students using speaking styles that are quite different from conversation. The non-native speaker of English who has advanced speaking skills must learn to use those skills in a new and different context.

Teaching a class is not like having a conversation with friends. English is used in some very different ways in teaching: Teachers usually have to talk louder than a speaker would in a conversation; teachers usually talk for longer stretches of time than anyone would in a conversation; the teacher is the person who is primarily responsible for keeping the talk going for the entire class period—that responsibility is shared with others in a conversation; the teacher is supposed to talk in highly organized ways rather than in the random and spontaneous fashion of conversation; the teacher's talk is supposed to help students understand the course content; the teacher's talk is supposed to be interesting to the students and to make them positively evaluate the results of the time spent listening to the teacher.

In addition, the human-relations skills needed by the teacher are different from those needed in conversations and in encounters with peers—or your own professors. Part Four includes activities for leading discussions and for stimulating student responses. At the same time that these activities are being practiced, you should be carrying out the observation activities in Part Five to find out more about how American undergraduates interact with their teachers at your institution.

One of the most important roles of the teacher is that of explainer. Part Four gives intensive, controlled practice in giving various types of explanations. The rigid limit of five minutes serves several purposes: You learn to be aware of time and to control it. You will find that longer lectures are usually best organized into a series of segments dealing with particular aspects of the larger topic. The severe time limit will also force you to think through your topic to arrive at the most effective and most direct explanation. That is, you practice the preferred American style of organization—getting right to the point.

As explained in Chapter 6, university instructors find that they repeatedly use the same types of explanations. These basic types are (1) definitions; (2a) descriptions of processes, (2b) descriptions of historical background, (2c) descriptions of systems and mechanisms (political, economic, etc., as well as mechanical); (3) explanations of reasons. A 50-minute presentation can easily be made up of four or five definitions, a description of a process, and an explanation of the reasons the process works as it does.

Short explanations have the same basic structure as other types of academic communication in English—introduction, body, and conclusion. You must tell the students what the explanation is about, give the explanation, and summarize at the end. The conclusion can also be a connecting statement that ties the explanation to another explanation.

The introductory statement clearly and explicitly tells your students what the explanation will be. This should take no more than one minute.

The body explains by giving definitions and examples to illustrate the topic. This should take about three minutes.

The conclusion indicates to the students that the explanation is over and reminds them of the importance of the information. It can also be a transition to the next explanation. This should take no more than one minute.

15.1 First Five-Minute Explanation

Pick out an important term from your field of study. It would be best to select something from a course like the one that you will be teaching. Plan a short and interesting explanation that defines the term to present to the class. You will have only five minutes to give the explanation. After four minutes, you will be warned that you have only one minute left. When the time is up, you must finish your sentence and stop. You can use the chalkboard, the overhead projector, or other audiovisual aids.

Assignment

1. Today you have ten minutes to make your plan. In the future, you will plan your explanations outside of class.

2. Present your explanation to the other members of the training course.

3. Evaluate your explanation using the evaluation sheets in 15.8. Discuss your evaluation with the teacher of the foreign teaching assistant training course.

Make your plan in the space provided below. List ideas and key words, but do not write complete sentences.

Introductory statement:
_____
_____
_____
_____
_____
_____

Body:
_____
_____
_____
_____
_____
_____

Conclusion:
_____
_____
_____
_____
_____
_____

15.2 Defining a Term

As discussed in Chapter 6, one of the most important tasks of the college and university teacher is to define basic terminology. In addition, the teacher helps the students learn how to use the terminology appropriately and to understand the reasons for learning these words.

Assignment

1. With the other members of the FTA training course, review the characteristics of a good explanation in 6.1.

2. Select a basic term from your field of study and plan an explanation that defines the term. Your explanation must last no more than five minutes.

3. Discuss the term that you are defining with another student in the training course, preferably someone from a different field of study. Talk over the organization that you are planning and the example(s) you will use.

4. Present your definition to the larger group.

5. Evaluate your explanation using the evaluation sheets in 15.8. Discuss your evaluation with the teacher of the training course.

15.3 Expanding on Definitions Given in the Text

Most introductory textbooks include many new terms and concepts that the students must understand in order to move to higher-level courses. Do the following assignment to better understand ways in which to analyze and develop definitions.

Assignment

1. With another student in the FTA training course, look through a chapter in a textbook used in your university in an introductory course. Find four terms that are defined in that chapter and then analyze the definitions. For example, how are they organized?

2. Compare these textbook definitions to dictionary definitions of the same words. How are they the same as or different from dictionary definitions?

3. Students expect teachers to be able to expand on the information given in the textbooks—not just to repeat what is available there. Talk with your partner about additional information that can be given to explain the terms you have selected from the introductory textbook. What additional example of or explanation for why the term is important can you give?

4. Select one of the four terms and present the expanded definition to the members of your FTA training course.

5. Evaluate the explanation using the evaluation sheets in 15.8.

15.4 Using Descriptions to Explain

As discussed in Chapter 6, teachers often use descriptions of objects, places, events, people, processes, and so forth, in explanations. Do the following assignment to learn more about using descriptive explanations.

Assignment

1. With the rest of the students in the FTA training course, first discuss what elements can be included in descriptions. Often a description tells what something looks like, but what does *look like* mean? Can other senses be included?

2. Working with another student, find a description in an introductory textbook to analyze together. How is the description organized? What senses are appealed to?

3. Compare your description to those of the other students in the training course. What different methods of organizing descriptions were found? Were there any differences in the senses appealed to based on the type of thing being described?

4. Select a topic that requires a description. Discuss with another student in the FTA training course the object, place, person, and so on, that you are planning to describe. Talk over the organization that you are planning and the information that you will use. The other person may have ideas that will help to improve your explanation. In addition, it usually helps to clarify your own ideas when you have to explain them to a peer.

5. Plan a five-minute explanation. You will give the talk in class. While you are giving the explanation, one of the participants will videotape you and another will act as timekeeper. You will be warned when four minutes are up. You must stop after five minutes. Plan for an audience of intelligent people who are not experts in your field.

6. Evaluate your explanation using the evaluation sheet in 15.8. Discuss your evaluation with the teacher of the training course.

15.5 Explanations That Give Reasons

To learn more about using reasons in explanations, do the following assignment.

Assignment

1. Select a topic that requires that you give reasons for something. In this type of explanation, you are answering the question *why*. For example,
   - Why did something happen in the past?
   - Why does some result happen in a particular situation?
   - Why is it important to know this particular information?
   - Why are these steps in the process important?
   - Why is it important not to do something?

2. To get ideas, either use the text that you are teaching or borrow from the departmental office a text that you might use in the future. In the first chapter, find a topic that requires the explanation of reasons. Show the topic to the teacher of the FTA training course for advice on handling it within the five-minute time limit.

3. Plan a five-minute explanation. While you are giving the explanation, one student will videotape you and another will act as timekeeper. You will be warned when four minutes are up. You must stop after five minutes. Plan for an audience of intelligent people who are not experts in your field.

4. Evaluate your explanation using the evaluation sheet in 15.8. Discuss your evaluation with the teacher of the training course.

15. 6 Using Conditional and Hypothetical Examples

Teachers use both conditional and hypothetical examples in academic explanations. In the first type, the teacher explains that under certain conditions certain results can be expected. For example, the teacher of mathematics or chemistry might use this type: "If you do such and such under such conditions, then you can expect such-and-such results." In the second type, the teacher imagines or hypothesizes what might happen if certain currently unreal or untrue events were to occur: "If the U.S. were to impose trade barriers, the Japanese reaction would be. . . ." Or, "If current levels of acid rain continue into the twenty-first century, one would expect. . . ." That is, the conditional involves certainty, whereas the hypothetical involves educated guessing. Do the following assignment to practice using conditional and hypothetical examples in your explanations.

Assignment

1. Select a statement of general truth or a physical law that is basic to your field of study. Illustrate that statement with a conditional example that shows how the generalization operates. Before presenting the information, share it with a member of the FTA training course to seek ways to improve your explanation. Then make the explanation for the entire group.

2. Work with another student in the FTA training course to decide on a hypothetical statement about the past. For example, if the government had done one thing (which it did not do), then what would have been the result (rather than what did happen). Discuss your ideas with the rest of the class.

3. Work with another student in the FTA training course to decide on a hypothetical statement about the future. For example, "If a nuclear war began between the Soviet Union and the U.S., the results for South America would include. . . ." Or, "If the current economic policies of . . . were to continue. . . ." Prepare a short explanation of the statement in which you explain two or three major implications of the hypothesis.

15. 7 A Longer Explanation of a Term

To a great extent, introductory courses teach low-level students the basic terminology that they need to participate in more advanced courses. That is, these students are learning new concepts and information *and* the technical vocabulary to be able to talk about the concepts and information. Therefore, teachers of introductory courses need to be excellent explainers of terminology and vocabulary.

Assignment

1. For your next lecture, you will have seven to ten minutes in which to explain a term or concept in your field. Keep in mind the following as you prepare your mini-lecture: Your audience is a freshman or sophomore class; they probably will not know very much about your field. In fact, this may be the first class they have ever taken in this subject. You should include some information about when or how the term or concept can be used in your field and how you will expect the students to be able to use it in the class. If possible, include examples to help make the term or concept understandable for your audience.

2. Evaluate your explanation using the evaluation sheets in 15.8. Discuss your evaluation with the teacher of the training course.

15.8 Evaluation of Explanations

It is important to learn from the explanations that you give and that you observe so that each experience makes you a better university instructor. The following evaluation sheet is based on the discussion of good explanations given in Chapter 6.

The characteristics of good explanations given in 6.3 can be used to evaluate many different kinds of explanations. You should keep 15.8 as the original and write only on a copy made for a particular evaluation activity. Ask the teacher of your foreign teaching assistant training course how many copies you will need for the activities planned for your course.

Explanation Evaluation Sheet

1. Use of Spoken Language

	OK	Needs Improvement
a. Sentences were not too long.		
b. Pauses were appropriate.		
c. Rate of speech was varied.		
d. Loudness of voice was varied.		
e. Voice was loud enough to be heard by all students.		
f. Voice was not too loud.		
g. Few grammar errors occurred.		
h. Key vocabulary was correctly pronounced.		
i. Questions from students were understood.		
j. Responses to questions were clear.		

Suggestions and Comments:

_____
_____
_____
_____
_____
_____
_____
_____

124 Chapter 15 *Learning to Give Short Explanations*

2. Use of Body Language

   a. Emphatic gestures were used.
   b. Eye contact was made with several students.
   c. Eye contact was regained after writing on board.

OK	Needs Improvement

Suggestions and Comments:

_____
_____
_____
_____

3. Relationship Skills
   a. Students were called on by name.
   b. Names of students who asked questions were known.
   c. The teacher smiled and seemed happy to be in class.
   d. The teacher seemed enthusiastic about subject matter.
   e. The teacher was courteous and respectful of students.

OK	Needs Improvement

Suggestions and Comments:

_____
_____
_____
_____

4. Lecturing Skill

	OK	Needs Improvement
a. Good examples were used.		
b. The purpose of the class was clearly stated.		
c. The topics being discussed were clearly stated.		
d. Good organization was exhibited.		
e. Organization was clearly stated.		
f. Few vague fillers were used.		
g. Formulas/Graphs were clearly presented.		
h. Key vocabulary was written on board.		
i. Organizing vocabulary was used to indicate relationships between parts of the explanation.		
j. Questions were answered accurately.		

Suggestions and Comments:

_____
_____
_____
_____
_____
_____
_____
_____
_____
_____
_____

126 Chapter 15 *Learning to Give Short Explanations*

15.9 Making a Transcript of an Audio Recording

It will be of value to you in improving your voice, teaching style, and lecture organization to make an audio recording that you then transcribe. This recording should be made in class and should be of one of the short explanations assigned in Part Four. After you have made the recording, you will take it home and transcribe it in detail. Then you will analyze your transcription according to the categories below.

1. In making your transcription, be sure to write down everything, including any false starts ("I think . . ."; "Well, let's . . ."), repetitions (of whole words or parts of words), pause fillers (such as *uh, um, er*, etc.), and any unfilled pauses. Indicate unfilled pauses by parentheses that include the approximate length of the unfilled pauses (short = 1 second or less; medium = 2–3 seconds; long = 4+ seconds). Skip a line between each line of written transcription. On these in-between lines, write comments about your voice quality, intonation, word stress, sentence rhythm, and pronunciation for the part of the lecture that you transcribed on the line above.

    Analyze your transcription for the following characteristics:

    No. of false starts _____   No. of repetitions _____

    No. of pause fillers _____   No. of unfilled pauses _____

    Avg. length of pause _____   Avg. no. of words between pauses _____

    Total no. of words* _____   Avg. no. of words per minute _____

    Most frequent word _____   No. of transition words _____

    Transition words used:

    _____   _____
    _____   _____
    _____   _____
    _____   _____
    _____   _____
    _____   _____

Voice Quality:

Intonation:

Word Stress:

Sentence Rhythm:

Pronunciation:

No. of Errors:

Content:

Vocabulary:

Organization:

2. Make another tape of the same or a different lecture, trying to improve on your first recording, based on your self-analysis.

*Each repetition, pause filler, and false start counts as a word.

Chapter • 16

Giving Mini-Lectures to Practice Particular Teaching Acts

♦ OVERVIEW

No matter what discipline you teach, you will find that you do certain general kinds of activities in the classroom. These common practices include introducing yourself to the students, making assignments, returning tests, and more. In this chapter, you will practice these typical teaching activities.

16.1 Introducing Yourself to a Class

The first day of class may be the most important day for the teacher because it is then that you introduce yourself to your students. Their first impression of your competence, communication skills, and human-relations skills will influence their attitudes toward you for many days to come. Thus, it is important to plan how to handle this teaching activity.

Assignment

1. You will have five minutes in which to introduce yourself as though it were the first day of class. You need to include the following information (not necessarily in the order in which it is given here):
   - The title and course number of the class
   - The text to be used and any additional material that students will be required to read and any supplies they may need
   - Your name
   - Your office number, office telephone number (if you have one), and the hours during which you will be available in your office
   - The requirements for the course (e.g., the number of tests and quizzes or lab sessions that must be completed and policies about late work, makeup exams, and so on)
   - Attendance policy
   - Basis on which the course grade will be computed

   Note: To guide your planning, get a copy of a sample course syllabus from your departmental office. That syllabus will show the kinds of information your institution requires each instructor to provide students. Most institutions require instructors to provide certain information in writing at the beginning of each course. In addition, most instructors discuss that information on the first day of class.

2. Evaluate your introduction to be sure that you included all of the required information.

16.2 Making Long-term Assignments

Very often you will include term projects as part of the requirements for a course. For example, students may be required to read a certain number of articles in journals and to write summaries of those articles. When making one of these assignments at the beginning of the term, you need to give students detailed instructions for completing the assignment.

Assignment

1. Plan a five-minute presentation in which you explain a term project. Arrange to have your presentation audiotaped or videotaped. Be sure to include at least the following:
   - The nature of the assignment (what exactly the students are supposed to do)
   - The purpose of the assignment (why you are asking them to do this)
   - The time limits (due date and policy on late completion)
   - The format of the completed assignment (typed, double-spaced, etc.)
   - Sources of information
   - Grading system and percentage of total grade for course
   - The kind of help that you are willing to give

   Note: Ask in your department's office for a sample syllabus for a course similar to the one you might teach. See if that syllabus suggests a term project. If so, then plan your presentation around that assignment.

2. Evaluate the audiotape or videotape of your presentation. Did you include all the necessary information? What changes might make your explanation easier to understand?

16.3 Making Short-term Assignments

You will often give your students short-term assignments—daily homework, for example.

Assignment

1. Plan a five-minute presentation in which you explain a homework assignment based on a textbook used in a course that you might teach. Be sure to include at least the following information:
   - What is the student supposed to do? (Read? Write? Answer questions? Be prepared to discuss?)
   - Why is the assignment being given?
   - When exactly is the assignment due?
   - What happens if the assignment is not done on time?
   - How will the assignment be graded? How is the grade figured into the total grade for the course?
   - What is the student supposed to give you—if anything?

You might again look at the sample syllabus from a course that you may teach. Or, you might ask a person who is currently teaching to share information about homework assignments given in that course.

2. To find out if your explanation was understood, ask questions of your "students" in the training course. For example, you could ask someone to repeat his/her understanding of the homework. Make additional explanation as necessary to be sure you and your students have the same ideas about the homework.

16.4 Announcing a Test

While all major tests should be included in your syllabus, it is not enough for most U.S. undergraduates to give them the syllabus at the beginning of the term and expect them to be prepared for a test. Most U.S. undergraduates expect the teacher to announce the test several class periods ahead of time and to discuss the details of the test then. They also expect that some reference will be made to the test in the class period immediately prior to the test ("Remember, we are having our midterm exam next class. Do you have any questions about it?").

Assignment

1. Plan a five-minute presentation in which you announce a test to your class. Arrange to have an audiotaped or videotaped recording made of your presentation. Include the following information in your presentation (though not necessarily in this order).
   - When will the test be given?
   - What is the purpose of the test?
   - What will be covered on the test?
   - What kinds of questions will be given (short answer, multiple choice, essay)? Approximately how many questions will be included?
   - How long will the test last (the whole period, part of the period)?
   - How will the test be graded? How will the grade fit into the total grade for the course?
   - When can the students expect to get the test papers back from you?

- What happens if someone does not take the test? (Will a makeup be given? What kinds of excuses are acceptable? You need to check departmental policy and traditions on this issue.)
- Are you willing to give any extra help during or in addition to your office hours while the students are preparing for the test? (Some teachers announce that they will answer questions about a test only in class, so that all students will receive the same information.)

2. Evaluate the tape of your presentation. Did you include all of the necessary information? What changes would you make the next time you announce a test?

16.5 Giving an Overview of a Unit

At the beginning of a new section or chapter of a text, it is sometimes useful to give the students an overview of the content and purposes of the unit before going into any detail about it.

Assignment

1. Plan a five-minute overview of a chapter in a text that you might teach. Include at least the following:

    - The organization of the unit (You might point out the importance of the title given the unit or any subtitles. This information can help the students understand the organization of the unit.)
    - The major purposes of the unit
    - The important terminology or key words that will be defined or emphasized
    - The types of activities that will be included (e.g., case studies, problems to be solved, or questions that will be answered)

2. Present the overview to another student in the FTA training course. Then listen to his/her overview. Discuss possible changes that might improve your presentations.

3. Present your overview to the whole group. Arrange to have it audiotaped or videotaped.

4. Discuss with your partner the differences between your two presentations. How was your presentation of the material to one person different from your presentation to the larger group?

16.6 Returning Tests

As you might remember from your own experience, getting a test back is a time of high emotion and tension for most students. Thus, it is especially important to handle this responsibility well.

Do not return the papers first and then try to talk generally about the test. Few of the students will be listening to you because they will be looking through their own papers and dealing with their own thoughts and emotions. Talk first and then give out the papers.

Assignment

1. Plan a three- to four-minute presentation in which you talk with the students about the test and the test papers before you return the papers to them. Arrange for your presentation to be audiotaped or videotaped. Include at least this information in your explanation:

    - Remind the students about the purpose of the test. ("I have your midterm exam papers here to return to you. You probably remember that the test included. . . .")
    - Remind them of the grading system for the course.
    - Explain how you have marked the papers. What symbols have you used, if any? What do your markings mean?
    - Explain the grading system and give an example of a grade.

- Explain how they can talk with you about any questions they might have about the marks or the grade. ("I'll stay after class to talk with you about questions. Also, my office hours are. . . . Or, you can make an appointment.")
- You might want to make a general remark about the papers. ("I was very pleased that most of you did so well on the test. You seem to understand the material well." Or, "A lot of you had trouble with question two on. . . . So, today we'll go back over that material as a review.")

2. In your observation of undergraduate classes in your department, have you seen how teachers return test papers? Describe their techniques. How did the students act? Did they ask any questions?

3. Evaluate the tape of your presentation. Did you include all the information?

16.7 Returning Homework

Most U.S. undergraduates have definite expectations about homework papers. They expect them to be returned promptly—within two or three class periods at the latest. They expect the teacher to be available to talk about any trouble they had with the work. They expect some use of class time when the papers are returned for a discussion of their work.

In fact, the returning of homework papers can be a good activity to use in building your relationships with the students. Some teachers come to class early to return homework; they use the time then to go over any problems that individual students might have had. In some fields such as mathematics, it is traditional to go over homework during the first part of class as a review and as a basis for the rest of the work that will be done.

Do not give out homework papers at the beginning of class and then try to start immediately into your lecture/discussion. Few of the students will be listening to you; they will be looking at their papers and trying to figure out how well they did.

Assignment

1. Discuss with the other participants in the FTA training course your observations of teacher and student behaviors when homework was returned. Was the homework used as part of the class? If so, how and for what purposes?

2. Plan a two- to three-minute presentation in which you talk with the students about the homework papers before giving them back. Arrange to audiotape or videotape your presentation. Include this kind of information:

   - Remind the students about the nature of the homework.
   - Remind them of your grading system and how the homework fits in.
   - Inform them in the case that everyone had trouble with a particular question and how you plan to deal with that question.
   - Tell them how they can arrange to meet with you if they have particular questions.
   - Tell them how you will deal with the papers right now. ("We'll take time now for you to look over your papers. Then we'll talk about question four since just about everyone had trouble with it." Or, "We'll take time now for you to look over your papers. If you have any questions, just raise your hand.")

3. Evaluate the tape of your performance. How did it compare with those you have observed in your department?

16.8 Supplementing Previous Explanations

16.8.a Corrections

On occasion you will realize that you have made a factual error during a presentation. In correcting the error, you have two concerns: first, you want your students to have correct information. Second, you want to maintain appropriate and effective relationships with your students. Thus, it is important to make the correction in a way that will not embarrass you or your students. Generally, a brief "I'm sorry but I gave you some wrong information" or "I'm sorry but I made a mistake" will be enough. Then give the correct information and ask questions to be sure that the students understand it.

Assignment

1. Work with another FTA to decide on an error of fact—for example, "2 + 2 = 5" or "the U.N. was founded in New York."

2. Then plan a brief correction in which you (a) apologize, (b) remind the students of what you had said, (c) give the correct information, and (d) ask questions that demonstrate that the students understand the corrected version of the facts.

3. Share your plan with the other participants in the FTA training course.

16.8.b Additions

You will find at times as you think about what happened in a class that the students' questions or reactions reveal that they did not understand your explanation. You might decide that the information is so important that you will need to return to it for part of the next class.

Assignment

1. Select some particular feature of a presentation that you gave earlier in the term. For example, you could select the definition of an important term.

2. Plan a five-minute presentation in which you return to the topic and explain it again using a different example or illustration. Be sure to include the following:

   - a reference to the previous class so that the students will understand that you are reviewing rather than presenting new material
   - the new version of the material
   - an opportunity for the students to ask questions or to answer questions so that you can be sure that they understood this new explanation.

3. Share your plan with the other participants in the FTA training course.

Chapter • 17

Learning to Give Longer Presentations

◆ OVERVIEW

In this chapter, you will use the skills gained earlier to build larger and longer presentations. Each of the longer explanations can be viewed as made up of related definitions, descriptions, and reason-giving explanations. Before giving these explanations, however, you will work to enhance your skills at analyzing the topics and textbook materials that are the basis for longer classes.

17.1 Analyzing a Topic

There is a tremendous difference between the kinds of things that students do to prepare for class and those that teachers do to prepare for class. Graduate teaching assistants are in the difficult position of being students during certain parts of each day and teachers in other parts. The preparation that you make for the classes you take includes (1) reading the required materials, (2) thinking about them, and (3) thinking about what the teacher might ask you to do in class. A teacher approaches the materials in a different way. The teacher must (1) analyze the materials to decide what is of primary importance, (2) think about what the students need to learn from the materials, (3) think about what the students might not know or might find hard to understand, (4) plan what he/she will say, and (5) plan methods for getting student input into the class (case-study discussion, discussion questions, etc.). Some textbooks include discussion questions at the end of each chapter. These questions can help you decide what the authors think are the major issues of the chapter. These textbook exercises and activities can also provide ideas for teaching methods that will give some variety to the class—discussion, problem solving, and so on, to use along with the lecture.

Assignment

1. Select a chapter from a textbook that you might teach. Identify the major points being made by the chapter.

2. Analyze each of those points—what terms must be understood or emphasized, what processes, what reasons.

3. Use the worksheet in 17.2 to write down your analysis.

4. After you have analyzed the text chapter, present a short explanation in your FTA training course in which you give your analysis of the topics covered in the chapter.

17.2 Worksheet for Analysis of Textbook Chapter

Copy this worksheet to use for this assignment so that you will be able to make additional copies to use when you are teaching.

1. Major topics (these might be suggested by the headings for the subdivisions of the chapter):

   a. _____
   b. _____
   c. _____
   d. _____
   e. _____
   f. _____
   g. _____
   h. _____
   i. _____
   j. _____

2. Terms to define or key words to emphasize:
   _____
   _____
   _____
   _____

3. Processes involved (if any):
   _____
   _____
   _____
   _____

4. Reasons involved (if any):
   _____
   _____
   _____
   _____

5. Background information that must be understood in order to comprehend the chapter (e.g., the linear equation might be needed to understand certain management principles):
   _____
   _____
   _____
   _____

6. Kinds of activities provided by the authors:
___
___
___
___
___
___

7. What information is of primary importance in this chapter?
___
___
___
___
___
___
___

8. What teaching methods can be used in dealing with this chapter? (Lecture, discussion, problem solving, etc.) Identify what material each teaching method would use.
___
___
___
___
___

9. What is a possible organization for a class period based on this chapter?
___
___
___
___
___
___
___
___

17.3 Describing a Process

For your next mini-lecture, you must explain a process (how to do something [active focus], how something is done [passive focus], or how something happens). Your audience is a group of undergraduates in an introductory course in your field. You can take up to fifteen minutes for this explanation. Arrange to have your mini-lectures videotaped.

Assignment

1. Your presentation should contain the following sections:

    a. In the introduction, identify the process. Define it; explain the meaning of the name of the process or of the term used to describe the process, if it is not self-explanatory or if it seems as though knowing the meaning of the name or term might help the students understand the process better. (This is a short definition explanation.)

    b. Tell what the process is used for, when it is used, and perhaps why it is used. (This explanation is basically for reason giving: why is this process explanation important to listen to and to learn?)

    c. Describe any equipment necessary to complete the process. (This section is a descriptive explanation.)

    d. Be sure to explain carefully any safety precautions. This can be a very important part of the presentation. (Again, this section involves a descriptive explanation, but it should also include reason giving—why the precautions are necessary.)

    e. Explain each step in the process thoroughly. Do not leave anything out. (This is a process explanation.)

    f. Explain the steps in a correct or appropriate order. (This is a continuation of *e*.)

    g. Signal when you are finished. (This is the conclusion.)

    h. Ask for questions. You should expect that there will be questions from the other students who are acting as your class.

2. Evaluate the tape of your explanation using the evaluation sheets in 15.8. Discuss your evaluation with the teacher of the training course.

17.4 Connecting One Lecture to Another

Teachers give coherence to courses and material by making references back to previous class sessions and by explaining how a particular class relates to future classes.

Assignment

1. For your next mini-lecture, you will give a 15-minute presentation. Your audience is assumed to be a group of undergraduates in the first course in the subject you are teaching, thus probably freshmen or sophomores who know little or nothing about the subject you are teaching. Arrange to have your mini-lectures videotaped.

2. In your presentation, you must do all of the following:

    a. Explain a concept or a procedure related to something you have explained in a previous speech. Indicate how what you are explaining now relates to what you explained earlier.

    b. Ask at least three questions of the class during the speech. You may use any of the question types you wish: rhetorical, information-seeking, clarifying, confirming. (See 6.8, 6.9, and 6.10 for information on questions.)

    c. Make an assignment for the next class period.

    d. Be prepared to be interrupted by questions during your presentation. You must appropriately handle any such questions.

3. Evaluate the tape of your explanation using the evaluation sheets in 15.8. Discuss your evaluation with the teacher of the training course.

17.5 Combining Definitions and Reason Giving

Longer lectures and presentations often combine definitions and explanations of the reasons for the importance of the defined terms.

1. Plan a 15-minute presentation in which you combine the giving of definitions with the giving of reasons. For example, you might give definitions of two or three related terms and then explain why these terms are important in your field of study. Be sure to give examples that illustrate how the terms function and why they are important.

    You could base this lecture on a chapter in a textbook that is used for a course you might teach. Select terms from the text and then explain the reasons that these concepts are important. Find your own examples to illustrate the terms and the reasons. That is, do not just repeat the examples given in the text. Your good students will know those examples and will expect you to be able to give additional information.

2. Plan to ask questions during this lecture. You can use any type of question that you like (see 6.8 for information on question types). Also, expect your students to interrupt with questions during the lecture. You must handle their questions appropriately.

3. Discuss your plans with another participant in the FTA training course. This discussion should help to clarify your organization and examples.

4. Arrange to have your presentation videotaped.

5. Evaluate the tape of your performance using the explanation evaluation sheets in 15.8.

17.6 Explaining a Cause-Effect Relationship

A major feature of teaching is to make students aware of the relationships among events and processes. In a chemistry class, for example, the teacher often will explain how one action in a particular situation with particular materials will lead to particular results. Other fields use this type of explanation, too.

Assignment

1. Plan a 15-minute explanation in which you explain an important cause-effect relationship in your field of study.

    Be sure to include the following:
    - any materials, events, or other elements that are involved
    - any characteristics of the required situation or environment
    - any actions that must be taken
    - the necessary sequencing of the actions
    - the reason this cause-effect relationship is important

2. Share your plans with another student to be sure that you are including the necessary information and that your explanation is well organized. It should have an introduction and a closing statement.

3. Make an audiotape of the presentation to analyze later. Evaluate the tape of your presentation to be sure that you included all of the necessary information. What changes would have made the cause-effect relationship clearer?

Chapter • 18

50-Minute Classes

◆ OVERVIEW

In the United States, we sometimes joke about the 50-minute hour. Few institutions have classes that are exactly 60 minutes long. The class periods range anywhere from 50 minutes for classes that meet five days a week to five hours for classes that meet once a week. In spite of those facts, we still tend to think of the basic class as lasting about one hour. (Longer classes are frequently divided into segments of about one hour with short breaks between the segments.) The core of these classes is usually a long lecture plus other class activities such as the giving of assignments or the returning of papers.

Since college or university instructors can expect to have to teach full 50-minute classes at some point, activities are included here in the analyzing, planning, and practicing for 50-minute classes.

18.1 Planning a 50-Minute Class

For this assignment, assume you are responsible for teaching a 50-minute lecture section in an introductory course in your department. To prepare for the lecture session, do the following assignment.

Assignment

1. Borrow a copy of the textbook for such an introductory course in your department and also try to get a copy of a typical syllabus for that course. Bring those materials to your FTA training course.

2. Working with another student, plan a 50-minute class based on one chapter of the textbook and on the syllabus.

3. Use the explanations given in Part Two of characteristics and organization of 50-minute classes. Also, use your observation experiences. The worksheet in 17.2 should be used to make notes about the content of the textbook chapter.

4. Share your plan with the rest of the group. Make adjustments based on the discussion.

18.2 Giving a 50-Minute Class

Present the class that you planned in 18.1. Arrange for it to be videotaped as well as audiotaped. View the tape with your teacher and with the student who helped you prepare. Use the evaluation sheets in 15.8 to guide your discussion.

Assignment

1. What things went well? List them.

2. Why do you think those things were so successful?

3. What things would you like to do differently next time? List them.

4. What makes you think these things need improvement?

5. How do you plan to make these changes?

18.3 Evaluation of a Faculty Member's Class

One way of improving your teaching is to observe and analyze the teaching of faculty in your department who are recognized as effective teachers. If possible, work with a group of students from your major department to do this activity.

Assignment

1. Find out through your department about undergraduate lecture courses being given by faculty (rather than by other graduate teaching assistants). Find out from other graduate students which of the professors has a reputation for being a good lecturer. Perhaps one of them has won a teaching award. Perhaps one of them has a reputation as an outstanding scholar but only a mediocre teacher.

2. After selecting the one who seems the most likely to be a good teacher, ask permission of the professor to attend some of his/her classes and to tape-record them. If the professor allows you to tape the class, take a tape recorder with a built-in microphone to record the classes for later analysis.

3. Use the observation sheets from Part Five to guide your observation of the teacher's manner and actions.

4. Use the explanation evaluation sheets (15.8) to analyze the effectiveness of the classes.

5. After analyzing the class, share your information with the other students in the training course, being careful to avoid hypercritical comments about the teacher you observed. Focus your discussion on things that you learned in your observation to improve your own teaching; you may have learned some positive things because of problems that the teacher had. ("I learned the importance of speaking loudly enough for the students in the back of the room to hear me.")

Chapter ◆ 19

Leading Discussions

◆ OVERVIEW

A teacher's responsibilities are different in leading discussions from those involved in presenting explanations (Chapter 8). The following activities will help you gain some of the skills needed to guide discussions successfully.

19.1 Phrases to Use in Guiding a Discussion

Getting students to participate in a discussion is an important skill for a university teacher. Various aspects of this skill are discussed in 3.1.c and Chapter 8. Teachers can learn to use certain phrases to guide the discussion. When using these guiding phrases, be sure to use the names of the students.

1. Phrases to get a discussion started (Insert a student's name in the slot at the beginning of the phrase to indicate to a particular student that the question is for him/her.)

    _____, would you summarize the case study for us?

    _____, how would you answer that question?

    _____, what are the points to consider in answering the question?

    _____, the textbook asks about. . . . What is the question getting at? What is the question about? What do the authors want us to think about?

2. Phrases to get other students involved

    _____, would you like to add anything?

    _____, would you like to add anything to that?

    _____, have we forgotten anything?

    _____, have we forgotten anything important?

    _____, what is your opinion?

    _____, how would you handle the situation?

    _____, do you agree with that approach?

    _____, do you agree with that answer?

    _____, would you like to add anything to the list of options/answers?

    _____, you told me that you work at. . . . How would they handle this situation?

    _____, what do you think the company should have done?

    _____, what do you think of that approach?

    _____, that's an interesting point. _____, what do you think? Would that approach work?

    _____, that's an interesting opinion. What evidence do you have for it?

3. Phrases to elicit summaries

    _____, would you list the answers we have so far?

    _____, would you please summarize the choices the company has in this situation?

    _____, would you summarize [_____] for us?

    Note: Some teachers get students involved by having one of the students write summaries of the discussion on the board rather than the teacher doing the writing. That way, the teacher can stay focused on the discussion instead of trying to listen and think and write all at the same time.

4. Phrases to control students who might talk too much.

    Thanks for your answer, _____. Let's see what _____ thinks.

    Thanks, _____. I'd like to find out what _____ thinks.

Assignment

1. Select a political or social topic that is currently important and being written about in the local newspaper and commented about on television.

2. Analyze the topic to select three major issues that are involved.

3. Plan a discussion during which you will get as many as possible of the members of the FTA training course to participate. Remember that your purpose is to get them to give their points of view and evidence to support those points of view. You are not responsible for any final answers about the topic; but rather your teaching responsibility is to give the students practice in presenting an idea and its support. They are also to practice the skill of polite academic disagreement during which many points of view can be discussed without personal animosity.

4. You will be evaluated on your ability to guide the discussion, to involve different students, and to get the students to present evidence for their opinions. You will be expected to use the names of the students during the discussion.

5. Plan to use phrases from all of the categories in guiding the discussion.

6. Evaluate the discussion using the sheet given in 19.5.

19. 2   Leading a Discussion of a Case Study

Some of you will need to learn to lead discussions on case studies—for example, in business or law. To prepare to lead a case-study discussion, the following steps have been found useful. After you thoroughly understand the case and its implications, then prepare for the discussion using the suggestions given in Chapter 8.

Steps to Understanding a Case Study

1. Read the case through quickly to get a general understanding.

2. Reread the case carefully a second time, perhaps outlining the major stages of presentation of the situation.

3. Identify the problems that are involved in the case. Write a list of the facts given about each problem, rereading the case to be sure that you have not forgotten any details.

4. Write a diagnosis of each case that indicates causes and results as well as the facts. If possible, divide the problems into major vs. minor.

5. Prepare a list of alternative solutions to each problem.

6. Evaluate the alternative solutions, listing the good and bad features of each.

7. Select the best solution and prepare a defense that compares the pros and cons of this solution with those of the other possible solutions.

Assignment

1. Select one of the case studies provided by your instructor or suggest one that is in a text you are teaching.

2. Analyze the case, using the worksheet that follows this assignment.

3. Then plan strategies for getting students to discuss the case so that they learn how to analyze a problem situation, develop alternatives, and select the best alternative for the particular situation.

4. When you lead the discussion, you will be evaluated on your ability to

   a. involve as many students as possible,
   b. get all of the major points discussed, and
   c. complete the discussion in 20–30 minutes.

5. Use the evaluation sheet given in 19.5.

19.3 Worksheet for Analyzing a Case Study

Make a copy of this worksheet to use for the assignment in 19.2. Save the original to make copies for later case-study analyses.

1. Outline of the major stages of the case

   _____
   _____
   _____
   _____
   _____

2. Problems and facts about each problem

   _____
   _____
   _____
   _____
   _____

3. Diagnosis that indicates causes and results

   _____
   _____
   _____
   _____

4. Major vs. minor problems

   _____
   _____
   _____
   _____

5. Alternative solutions for each problem with good and bad features of each

   _____
   _____
   _____
   _____
   _____

6. Best solution with its pros and cons

   _____
   _____
   _____
   _____

Chapter 19 *Leading Discussions*   147

19. 4 Leading a Discussion of an Explanation

The teacher of the foreign teaching assistant training course will arrange for each class member to have a copy of a textbook or a representative chapter of the book that is used in an introductory course that you might teach. All of the other students in the training course will read the same chapter to prepare for a discussion of the questions given at the end of the chapter. Your responsibility will be to prepare to lead the discussion.

Assignment

1. Answer the questions at the end of the chapter. What are the important points that the questions are designed to bring out?

2. Plan questions and statements that you will use to start the discussion. Decide on particular students that you will direct these questions to.

3. Think about time limits. How much time can you allow for each question? (This discussion should take about 15 minutes.)

4. Evaluate your leading of the discussion using the evaluation sheet given in 19.5.

19.5 Evaluation Sheet for Discussions

Make copies of this evaluation sheet for later use.

Yes	No	
____	____	1. The teacher kept the focus on the students.
____	____	2. The teacher got many different students involved in the discussion.
____	____	3. All the major points were covered.
____	____	4. No one student dominated the discussion.
____	____	5. The teacher used guiding statements to direct the flow of the discussion.
____	____	6. The teacher controlled the time for the discussion accurately.
____	____	7. The teacher got the students to give evidence for their answers and points of view.

Suggestions and Comments:

_____
_____
_____
_____
_____
_____
_____
_____
_____
_____

Chapter ♦ 20

Explaining by Doing

♦ OVERVIEW

University teachers not only make presentations about concepts; they also often demonstrate processes. For example, mathematics teachers show students how to solve problems, and chemistry teachers lead students in learning how to carry out experimental procedures. The activities in this chapter will help you develop your skills in this important teaching technique.

20.1 An Example From the Teaching of Mathematics

In introductory courses in mathematics, the usual method of instruction involves the solving of selected problems on the chalkboard while the instructor talks about what he/she is doing. The instructor is expected to explain any special difficulties and any special methods (or "tricks") that might be used in dealing with the problem. This type of teaching is much more difficult than it might appear at first. The teacher is expected to clarify a problem that is a model for other problems the students can expect to deal with later. In addition, this type of instruction can be difficult for a non-native speaker of English because the teacher must write, talk, listen, and think at the same time.

Assignment

1. Arrange to visit an introductory class in mathematics that is taught by a faculty member who is a native speaker of American English.

2. Use Observations Sheets 22.2, 22.3, 22.4, and 22.5 to guide your observations about the ways the English language is used to explain the materials. You might notice that a large portion of the class is actually taught in everyday English rather than in the language of mathematics as the teacher explains the materials to beginning students.

3. Notice how the teacher uses the chalkboard. Can his/her writing be read from the back of the room? At what points does he/she erase material from the board? What kind of information is written on the board in addition to the mathematical problem?

4. Discuss your observations with the other members of the FTA training course.

20.2 Using Formulas in Other Fields

Teachers in many different fields of study can find it important to explain a mathematical formula well. For example, a management or finance instructor might find it important to show how the linear equation has been applied in business or economics.

Assignment

1. Select a mathematical formula or formulas used in your field of study in introductory courses. Plan a 15-minute explanation of the formula(s). Be sure to include information on

    - the reasons the formula(s) is important
    - the concepts that are being explained by the formula(s)
    - the vocabulary that is necessary to talk about the formula(s)
    - the exact form of the formula(s)
    - practical examples of how the formula(s) can apply in your field of study

    You might review 7.1 on using the chalkboard well. It is especially important in teaching introductory courses not to use abbreviations that are unfamiliar to the students. Write out the full forms of the terms before using the abbreviations. You might have observed that many American undergraduates have weak backgrounds in mathematics, so it would be better not to preface presentations of formulas with comments about how easy they are since they may not appear easy to your students.

2. Present your presentation to the FTA training course. Arrange to have the presentation videotaped. Analyze your presentation to be sure you included all the necessary information. Also evaluate your use of the chalkboard.

Part FIVE
OBSERVATION

Chapter • 21

Observation of Classroom Space

♦ OVERVIEW

Observation activities will help you learn about the various interaction styles and communication strategies used by teachers and students in the U.S. classroom. You should think of yourself as an anthropologist entering a strange new land and attempting to use all your powers of observation and analysis to understand what is happening and how these people are communicating.

For each observation sheet, you should observe a different class period or part of a period. The teacher of your foreign teaching assistant training course will tell you how many copies of each observation sheet you will need to make.

21.1 Observation of the Classroom Space Used for a Graduate Course

Use this sheet to observe closely the space in which you are taking an advanced graduate course.

Observer's Name: _____

Course Observed: _____

Type of Class (lecture, lab, etc.): _____

Date: _____ Time: _____

Instructor's Name: _____

The room

a. Size: _____

b. Shape: _____

c. Lighting: _____

d. Temperature: _____

e. Seating arrangement: _____

f. Number of chairs available for students: _____

g. Location of the teaching area: _____

h. Location of the instructor: _____

i. Audiovisual equipment available: _____

_____

21.2 Observation of the Classroom Space Used for an Undergraduate Course

Use this sheet to observe closely the classroom in which a section of a required undergraduate course is taught.

Observer's Name: _____

Course Observed: _____

Type of Class (lecture, lab, etc.): _____

Date: _____ Time: _____

Instructor's Name: _____

1. The room

   a. Size: _____

   b. Shape: _____

   c. Lighting: _____

   d. Temperature: _____

   e. Seating arrangement: _____

   f. Number of chairs available for students: _____

   g. Location of the teaching area: _____

   h. Location of the instructor: _____

   i. Audiovisual equipment available: _____
   _____

2. Compare this room with the room used for the graduate course described in 21.1. What are the major differences? What differences in educational purposes are reflected in differences in space?

Chapter ◆ 22

Observation of Teaching Behaviors

◆ OVERVIEW

One of the most effective ways of learning about teaching methods preferred in your department is to observe the teaching of a faculty member who is noted for skillful teaching. The following observation sheets will help you to focus on different aspects of the teacher's behavior.

22.1 Observation of the Instructor

Observer's Name: _____

Course Observed: _____

Type of Class (lecture, lab, etc.): _____

Date: _____ Time: _____

Instructor's Name: _____

1. What was the instructor wearing?
   _____
   _____
   _____
   _____

2. What did the instructor do from the time he/she entered the room until the class began?
   _____
   _____
   _____
   _____

3. How did the instructor signal that the class would begin?
   _____
   _____
   _____
   _____

4. Language activities: What did the instructor do in each of these language categories? What percentage of class time was devoted to each type of activity?

   a. Reading:
   _____
   _____
   _____
   _____

   b. Speaking:
   _____
   _____
   _____
   _____

158   Chapter 22   *Observation of Teaching Behaviors*

    c. Writing:

    d. Listening:

5. How did the instructor signal that the class was finished?

6. What did the instructor do from the time the class finished until he/she left the room?

22.2 Observation of Instructor's Language Acts

Observer's Name: _____

Course Observed: _____

Type of Class (lecture, lab, etc.): _____

Date: _____ Time: _____

Instructor's Name: _____

During any class, a teacher will use many different kinds of communication. Observe those used by the teacher in this class. Think about ways of using these in your lecturing to improve clarity and intelligibility.

Circle the appropriate answer; put comments in the space provided.

1. Speaking: What type of speaking was done?

    a. To entire class: Yes / No

    _____
    _____
    _____
    _____

    b. To individual students (when? why? how many times?): Yes / No

    _____
    _____
    _____
    _____

    c. To self (when? why? how many times?): Yes / No

    _____
    _____
    _____
    _____

2. Reading: What kind of reading was done? Did the instructor read aloud to the whole class or to an individual student? Did he/she read silently?

    a. From textbook: Yes / No

    _____
    _____
    _____
    _____

b. From magazine or newspaper: Yes / No

c. From overhead projected image: Yes / No

d. From the roll book: Yes / No

e. Other: What other kinds of materials did the instructor read?

3. Writing: What kinds of writing did the teacher do?
   a. On chalkboard: Yes / No

   b. On overhead transparency: Yes / No

c. Other: What other kinds of writing did the instructor do during the class?
_____
_____
_____

d. Was the writing easy to read? If not, why not? How would you suggest that he/she improve the clarity of this communication?
_____
_____
_____
_____

4. Listening: What listening did the teacher do? Was there any pattern to this listening—more to students in the front of the room than in the back of the room, for example?

   a. To student questions: Yes / No
   _____
   _____
   _____
   _____

   b. To student answers to the teacher's questions: Yes / No
   _____
   _____
   _____

   c. To prerecorded materials (what kinds?): Yes / No
   _____
   _____
   _____
   _____

22.3 Observation of the Instructor's Nonverbal Acts

Observer's Name: _____

Course Observed: _____

Type of Class (lecture, lab, etc.): _____

Date: _____ Time: _____

Instructor's Name: _____

Teachers move around during their lectures. They move their bodies and their hands. Observe this teacher's actions in detail and write down how many times and for how long the teacher made each of the kinds of movements indicated. (See 6.7 for more information on nonverbal communication.)

Make notes on the number of times the action occurs and how long it lasts. Space is also provided for comments on the influence of the nonverbal actions on the instructor's effectiveness as a speaker and teacher.

1. Movement:

   a. Walking around

   _____
   _____
   _____
   _____

   b. Standing behind podium/desk

   _____
   _____
   _____
   _____

   c. Walking to chalkboard

   _____
   _____
   _____
   _____

   d. Walking back to look at what is written on the chalkboard

   _____
   _____
   _____
   _____

e. Moving away from the front-and-center position
_____
_____
_____
_____

f. Sitting down (where?)
_____
_____
_____
_____

2. Gestures with hands and face
   a. Pointing (at what? at whom? which finger?)
   _____
   _____
   _____
   _____

   b. Making a fist
   _____
   _____
   _____
   _____

   c. Making a stop gesture with palm
   _____
   _____
   _____
   _____

   d. Gestures to indicate growth or expansion
   _____
   _____
   _____
   _____

e. Gestures to indicate shrinking or loss

f. Taking glasses off/putting glasses on

g. Touching own body (where? what seemed to be meant—if anything?)

h. Other hand gestures (what gestures for what meanings?)

i. Raising eyebrows

j. Other facial gestures

3. Other physical actions
   a. Writing on chalkboard

   b. Writing on overhead transparency

   c. Flipping sheets of notes

   d. Other writing

   e. Other physical actions

22.4 Observation of the Use of Organizing Language

Observer's Name: _____

Course Observed: _____

Type of Class (lecture, lab, etc.): _____

Date: _____ Time: _____

Instructor's Name: _____

In the list of characteristics of good explainers and explanations in Chapter 6, one of the features is that they use "organizing vocabulary to indicate relationships between parts of the explanation." This statement means that good explainers use words and phrases such as *first, next, at the beginning of this discussion, earlier I gave the definition for* _____, *and so on*.

Write down any words or phrases used by the teacher in the class that you are observing to show the students the organization of the explanation.

_____
_____
_____
_____
_____
_____
_____
_____
_____
_____
_____
_____
_____
_____
_____
_____
_____
_____

22.5 Observation of the Use of Purpose Statements

Observer's Name: _____

Course Observed: _____

Type of Class (lecture, lab, etc.): _____

Date: _____ Time: _____

Instructor's Name: _____

Teachers frequently use phrases that tell the students the purposes of the class: "Today, we will _____." "The purpose of this class is _____."

Observe a class to see the use of these purpose statements by the teacher. Write down the exact words used by the teacher to tell the students the purpose of the class. Be sure to include anything said at the end of the class in the summary.

_____
_____
_____
_____
_____
_____
_____
_____
_____
_____
_____
_____
_____
_____
_____
_____
_____
_____
_____
_____

22.6 Observation of the Use of Audience-Inclusive Language

Observer's Name: _____

Course Observed: _____

Type of Class (lecture, lab, etc.): _____

Date: _____ Time: _____

Instructor's Name: _____

Teachers frequently use words and phrases to indicate to the students that they and the students are working together to achieve the goals of the course, for example, "Let's begin by _____." "We have lots to do before the break."

This sheet will help you observe such audience-inclusive language used in an undergraduate class like one that you might teach. Write down any such language used by the teacher.

1. List the words and phrases here.

_____
_____
_____
_____
_____
_____
_____
_____

2. At what points in the class did the teacher use this language—at the beginning, when introducing problems or homework, and so on?

_____
_____
_____
_____
_____
_____
_____
_____

Chapter ♦ 23

Observation of Student Behaviors

♦ OVERVIEW

Effective teaching involves both knowledge of your content area and understanding of the needs and behaviors of the students in your classes. The following observation sheets help you focus on different aspects of the classroom behavior of U.S. undergraduate students.

23.1 General Observation of Students

Observer's Name: _____

Course Observed: _____

Type of Class (lecture, lab, etc.): _____

Date: _____ Time: _____

Instructor's Name: _____

1. What sorts of clothes were the students wearing?
   _____
   _____
   _____
   _____

2. What did the students do from the time they came into the room until class started?
   _____
   _____
   _____
   _____

3. Did any students come into the class after it had started? What did they do as they entered?
   _____
   _____
   _____
   _____

4. What activities did the students engage in during the class? How much time did they spend on each activity?

   a. Reading:
   _____
   _____

   b. Speaking:
   _____
   _____

c. Writing:
_____
_____

d. Listening:
_____
_____

5. How did students indicate that they were interested?
_____
_____
_____

6. How did students indicate that they were bored?
_____
_____
_____

7. What did the students do to indicate that they thought the class was about to end?
_____
_____
_____

8. What did the students do when the teacher announced that the class was finished?
_____
_____
_____

23.2 Observation of One Particular Student

Observer's Name: _____

Course Observed: _____

Type of Class (lecture, lab, etc.): _____

Date: _____ Time: _____

Instructor's Name: _____

Select one student to watch carefully. What did he/she do during the class? Write descriptions here of his/her behavior.

1. What sort of clothes was the student wearing?
_____
_____
_____

2. What did the student do from the time he/she came into the room until class started?
_____
_____
_____

3. Did this student come into the class after it had started? What did he/she do upon entering the room?
_____
_____
_____

4. What activities did the student engage in during the class? How much time did he/she spend on each activity?

  a. Reading:
_____
_____
_____

  b. Speaking:
_____
_____
_____

c. Writing:
___
___
___

d. Listening:
___
___
___

5. Did the student indicate that he/she was interested? How?
___
___
___

6. Did the student indicate that he/she was bored? How?
___
___
___

7. What did the student do to indicate that he/she thought the class was about to end?
___
___
___

8. What did the student do when the teacher announced that the class was finished?
___
___
___

23.3 Observation and Comparison of Three Types of Students

Observer's Name: _____

Course Observed: _____

Type of Class (lecture, lab, etc.): _____

Date: _____ Time: _____

Instructor's Name: _____

Select three students to observe. One should be in the front part of the room; the second, in the middle; and the third, in the back. Watch each for two minutes at the beginning, the middle, and the end of the class period.

Student #1:

List characteristics of appearance:
_____
_____
_____

1. Check behaviors during the first part of the class:
   a. Listening ____
   b. Asking questions ____
   c. Writing in notebook ____
   d. Looking at the teacher ____
   e. Talking with friend ____
   f. Moving body around a lot ____
   g. Reading in textbook ____
   h. Reading something else ____ what? _____
   i. Sleeping ____
   j. Other ____ what? _____

2. Check behaviors during the middle of the class:
   a. Listening ____
   b. Asking questions ____
   c. Writing in notebook ____
   d. Looking at the teacher ____
   e. Talking with friend ____
   f. Moving body around a lot ____
   g. Reading in textbook ____
   h. Reading something else ____ what? _____

i. Sleeping ____
j. Other ____ what? _____

3. Check behaviors during the last part of the class:
   a. Listening ____
   b. Asking questions ____
   c. Writing in notebook ____
   d. Looking at the teacher ____
   e. Talking with friend ____
   f. Moving body around a lot ____
   g. Reading in textbook ____
   h. Reading something else ____ what? _____
   i. Sleeping ____
   j. Other ____ what? _____

Student #2:

List characteristics of appearance:
_____
_____
_____

1. Check behaviors during the first part of the class:
   a. Listening ____
   b. Asking questions ____
   c. Writing in notebook ____
   d. Looking at the teacher ____
   e. Talking with friend ____
   f. Moving body around a lot ____
   g. Reading in textbook ____
   h. Reading something else ____ what? _____
   i. Sleeping ____
   j. Other ____ what? _____

2. Check behaviors during the middle of the class:
   a. Listening ____
   b. Asking questions ____
   c. Writing in notebook ____
   d. Looking at the teacher ____
   e. Talking with friend ____

Chapter 23 Observation of Student Behaviors

   f. Moving body around a lot ____
   g. Reading in textbook ____
   h. Reading something else ____ what? _____
   i. Sleeping ____
   j. Other ____ what? _____

3. Check behaviors during the last part of the class:
   a. Listening ____
   b. Asking questions ____
   c. Writing in notebook ____
   d. Looking at the teacher ____
   e. Talking with friend ____
   f. Moving body around a lot ____
   g. Reading in textbook ____
   h. Reading something else ____ what? _____
   i. Sleeping ____
   j. Other ____ what? _____

Student #3:

List characteristics of appearance:

_____
_____
_____

1. Check behaviors during the first part of the class:
   a. Listening ____
   b. Asking questions ____
   c. Writing in notebook ____
   d. Looking at the teacher ____
   e. Talking with friend ____
   f. Moving body around a lot ____
   g. Reading in textbook ____
   h. Reading something else ____ what? _____
   i. Sleeping ____
   j. Other ____ what? _____

2. Check behaviors during the middle of the class:
   a. Listening ____
   b. Asking questions ____

c. Writing in notebook ____
d. Looking at the teacher ____
e. Talking with friend ____
f. Moving body around a lot ____
g. Reading in textbook ____
h. Reading something else ____ what? _____
i. Sleeping ____
j. Other ____ what? _____

3. Check behaviors during the last part of the class:
   a. Listening ____
   b. Asking questions ____
   c. Writing in notebook ____
   d. Looking at the teacher ____
   e. Talking with friend ____
   f. Moving body around a lot ____
   g. Reading in textbook ____
   h. Reading something else ____ what? _____
   i. Sleeping ____
   j. Other ____ what? _____

Assignment

1. Are there any differences in the behavior of the three students? If so, list and explain them.
   _____
   _____
   _____
   _____
   _____
   _____
   _____
   _____
   _____
   _____
   _____
   _____

2. Share your analysis with other participants in your FTA training course.

Chapter ♦ 24

Observation of Use of Questions by Teachers and Students

♦ OVERVIEW

As pointed out in 3.1.b, 6.8, and 6.10, many effective teachers find that they can use various types of questions to help their students learn. In addition, an important skill for a teacher is the ability to interpret student comments and questions correctly so that the student receives the information and help he/she is seeking. The observation sheets in Chapter 24 are designed to help you focus on the questioning that occurs in classroom settings.

24.1 Observation of Student Questions

Observer's Name: _____

Course Observed: _____

Type of Class (lecture, lab, etc.): _____

Date: _____ Time: _____

Instructor's Name: _____

Sometimes questions are in the traditional form of grammatical questions. Sometimes questions are indicated only by tone of voice or are indicated only by context. Review the question types discussed in 6.9 and 6.10 before observing an undergraduate class like the one that you might teach. During this observation, write down the exact words spoken by students in asking questions. It would probably be best both to take notes during class and to tape-record the class. Then use your tape to check and correct the notes.

In this space, write the exact words used by students to ask questions.

24.2 Observation of Question Interactions

Use the tape that you made in 24.1. Analyze the interactions between the students and the teacher. Review the discussion of the use of questions in 6.8.

Assignment

1. In the space provided below, write down the teacher's exact response to each question asked.

2. Then, analyze the appropriateness of the response.

3. Did the teacher understand what was asked?

4. Did the teacher actually answer the question?

5. What did the teacher do if he/she did not understand the question?

6. Share your analysis with the other participants in the training course.

24.3 Observation of Teacher Questions

Observer's Name: _____

Course Observed: _____

Type of Class (lecture, lab, etc.): _____

Date: _____ Time: _____

Instructor's Name: _____

As shown in 6.8, 6.9, and 6.10, teachers ask questions in a variety of ways and for a variety of purposes. Write down the exact words spoken by the teacher that seem to indicate that the teacher is asking questions of students during this class. It would probably be best both to take notes during class and to tape-record the class. Then use your tape to check and correct the notes. Write the teacher's question and the student's response in the space provided below.

Teacher's Question	Student's Response

182 Chapter 24 *Observation of Use of Questions by Teachers and Students*

24.4 Observation of Types and Purposes of Questions

Observer's Name: _____

Course Observed: _____

Type of Class (lecture, lab, etc.): _____

Date: _____ Time: _____

Instructor's Name: _____

Often teachers ask questions of students in ways that may not sound like questions. You probably recorded some of these questions that do not sound like questions in the previous observation. For this observation, you will need to concentrate on the various forms in which questioning may be done.

1. Write down the examples of the teacher's words under each of the following categories.

   a. Questions using grammatical word order for questions:

   ("John, what is the answer to question 1?" "What would one expect to be the result of Roosevelt's economic policies?")

   _____
   _____
   _____
   _____

   b. Questions using statement order but rising intonation:

   ("Mary, you have a question?" "All of you know where we are in the text?")

   _____
   _____
   _____
   _____

   c. Questions that use the imperative sentence form:

   ("Jack, give us the answer, please.")

   _____
   _____
   _____
   _____

   d. Questions that were purposefully incorrect statements:

   ("So 2 + 2 equals 6, right?")

   _____
   _____
   _____
   _____

e. Questions that involved incomplete statements:

("John, the answer to the problem is. . . .")
___

2. Now analyze the purposes for each question. Number each of the questions so that they will be easier to refer to. Then put the number of each question in the blank space that corresponds to its purpose.

   a. These questions were used to seek information:
   ___

   b. These questions were used to check student understanding:
   ___

   c. These questions were used to clarify a statement or a question for a student:
   ___

   d. These questions were rhetorical (used to indicate what the instructor was going to talk about):
   ___

3. Share your results with other participants in the FTA training course.

24.5 Observation of the Use of Clarifying Questions

Observer's Name: _____

Course Observed: _____

Type of Class (lecture, lab, etc.): _____

Date: _____ Time: _____

Instructor's Name: _____

In American classrooms, teachers and students often ask each other questions. As you saw in earlier observations, there are many ways of asking questions. Sometimes the teacher is not sure exactly what the student wants to know or why the student is asking the question. During your observations, watch for an occasion on which the teacher deals with a student question that he/she does not understand. Here is an example of the type of encounter you are looking for:

> Student: "Mmmmmm."
> Teacher: "I'm sorry, Mary. I couldn't hear you."
> Student: "Would you repeat mmmm."
> Teacher: "Which one did you want repeated?"
> Student: "Number 2."
> Teacher: "OK, number 2 was. . . ."

1. Write down the exact words used in the encounter: what does the teacher say? What does the student say? Also, make notes on the actions and body language of the teacher.

2. Analyze what occurred during the encounter. For example, the teacher did not understand what the student said. Or, the teacher understood what the student said but was not sure what the student wanted to know.

3. Working with the other students in the FTA training course, develop a list of the methods used by American teachers to clarify students' questions. Write that list here for later reference.

_____
_____
_____
_____
_____
_____
_____
_____
_____
_____
_____
_____
_____
_____
_____
_____

24.6 Signals That Indicate Question Types Used by Students

After reviewing the question types discussed in 6.9 and 6.10, observe an undergraduate class in your department and think about other classes that you have observed.

What verbal and nonverbal signals are given by students to indicate the type of question being asked? For example, a student might say, "That's on page 217?" If the teacher had just given the page number, the student is verbally asking for clarification. It is also possible that the teacher might notice a puzzled look on the student's face that is a nonverbal request for clarification.

What are some of the signals of the following types of classroom questions?

1. Check for understanding

2. Request for clarification

3. Request for further information

4. Disagreement with the teacher's statement

5. Disagreement with another student's statement

6. Challenge to the teacher's authority

7. Challenge to the textbook's authority

8. Getting off the track

9. Frivolous question

10. Disruptive question

Chapter ♦ 25

Overall Observation of Classes

♦ OVERVIEW

The observation sheets in Chapter 25 are designed to help you take an overall look at two different undergraduate classes and then compare teaching styles and student behaviors in two different academic fields.

Chapter 25 *Overall Observation of Classes* 187

25.1 Observing a Class for the First Time

Observer's Name: _____

Course Observed: _____

Type of Class (lecture, lab, etc.): _____

Date: _____ Time: _____

Instructor's Name: _____

Attend a section of an undergraduate course in your department that you have not observed before. Use this sheet to get a general impression of the teacher, the students, and their interaction as a class.

1. Lecture
   a. Main topic:
   _____
   _____

   b. Major points:
   _____
   _____

   c. Audiovisual equipment used:
   _____
   _____

2. Teaching Activities: What did the teacher do in each of these language categories?
   a. Reading:
   _____
   _____

   b. Speaking:
   _____
   _____

   c. Writing:
   _____
   _____

   d. Listening:
   _____
   _____

3. Student Activities: What did the students do in each of these categories?

   a. Reading:
   _____
   _____

   b. Speaking:
   _____
   _____

   c. Writing:
   _____
   _____
   _____

   d. Listening:
   _____
   _____
   _____

4. The Room

   a. Size:
   _____

   b. Shape:
   _____

   c. Lighting:
   _____

   d. Seating arrangement:
   _____

   e. Location of the teaching area:
   _____

5. Select one student to watch carefully. What did he/she do during class? Write descriptions here of his/her behavior.
   _____
   _____
   _____
   _____
   _____
   _____

6. Observation questions
   a. How did the teacher signal that he/she was ready to start class?
   _____
   _____
   _____

   b. How did the students indicate that they were interested?
   _____
   _____
   _____

   c. How did the students indicate that they were bored?
   _____
   _____
   _____

   d. What did the students do during the class?
   _____
   _____
   _____

   e. What did the students do to indicate that they thought the class was soon to end?
   _____
   _____
   _____

   f. What did the teacher do to indicate that the class was over?
   _____
   _____
   _____

   g. What happened immediately after the class ended?
   _____
   _____
   _____

25.2 Observation of a Class in a Different Department

Observer's Name: _____

Course Observed: _____

Type of Class (lecture, lab, etc.): _____

Date: _____ Time: _____

Instructor's Name: _____

With the help of one of your colleagues in the training course, visit an undergraduate section in a department other than your own. Try to find something as different from your discipline as possible.

1. Lecture
   a. Main topic:
   _____
   _____

   b. Major points:
   _____
   _____

   c. Audiovisual equipment used:
   _____
   _____

2. Teaching Activities: What did the teacher do in each of these language categories?
   a. Reading:
   _____
   _____
   _____
   _____

   b. Speaking:
   _____
   _____
   _____
   _____

   c. Writing:
   _____
   _____
   _____
   _____

d. Listening:
_____
_____
_____
_____

3. Student Activities: What did the students do in each of these categories?
   a. Reading:
   _____
   _____
   _____
   _____

   b. Speaking:
   _____
   _____
   _____
   _____

   c. Writing:
   _____
   _____
   _____
   _____

   d. Listening:
   _____
   _____
   _____
   _____

4. The Room
   a. Size:
   _____

   b. Shape:
   _____

   c. Lighting:
   _____

d. Seating arrangement:
_____

e. Location of the teaching area:
_____

5. Select one student to watch carefully. What did he/she do during class? Write descriptions here of his/her behavior.
_____
_____
_____
_____
_____
_____
_____
_____

6. Observation questions

   a. How did the teacher signal that he/she was ready to start class?
   _____
   _____
   _____

   b. How did the students indicate that they were interested?
   _____
   _____
   _____

   c. How did the students indicate that they were bored?
   _____
   _____
   _____

   d. What did the students do during the class?
   _____
   _____
   _____

e. What did the students do to indicate that they thought the class was soon to end?
___
___
___

f. What did the teacher do to indicate that the class was over?
___
___
___

g. What happened immediately after the class ended?
___
___
___

7. Compare the class in observation 25.1 with the class observed in 25.2. How are teachers, students, and classes observably alike and different in the two different departments observed in these activities?

Similarities

___
___
___
___
___
___
___
___

Differences

___
___
___
___
___
___
___
___

APPENDIX

The five parts of the *Foreign Teaching Assistant's Manual* are planned for integration into a course that fits the needs of a particular institution. The course designer selects materials and activities based on the length of the course, the teaching assignments of the graduate students, the language skills of those students, along with numerous other factors. The following cross-referencing suggests combinations of materials that might be used in a training program. No cross-references are given to the spoken English activities in Part Three because we expect these materials to be used consistently across the whole of the training course, based on the particular needs of the graduate students in the course. Thus, the graduate students will be discussing backgrounds, observing classes, learning about teaching behaviors, planning presentations, and practicing various teaching acts in a pattern that starts with background discussions but does not wait until the end of the course before beginning practical applications.

1. Materials and activities that focus on the roles and behaviors of U.S. faculty include "Analysis of Faculty Roles and Behaviors" (1.5, 1.6); Chapter 2, "Departmental Relations"; Chapter 4, "Profiles of Teachers in American Colleges and Universities"; Part 2, "Background to Teaching"; Chapter 22, "Observation of Teaching Behaviors"; Chapter 24, "Observation of Use of Questions by Teachers and Students"; and Chapter 25, "Overall Observation of Classes."
2. Materials and activities that focus on the roles and behaviors of U.S. undergraduate students include "Analysis of Student Roles and Behaviors" (1.7, 1.8); Chapter 3, "Profiles of American Students"; Chapter 23, "Observation of Student Behaviors"; Chapter 24, "Observation of Use of Questions by Teachers and Students"; and Chapter 25, "Overall Observation of Classes."
3. Chapter 5, "Planning and Organizing the Course," can be used along with "In the Classroom" (4.1).
4. Materials and activities that focus on the act of teaching include "In the Classroom" (4.1, 4.2); Chapter 6, "Presenting in Class or Lab"; Chapter 7, "Using Audiovisual Aids"; Chapter 8, "Leading a Discussion"; Chapter 15, "Learning to Give Short Explanations"; Chapter 16, "Giving Mini-Lectures to Practice Particular Teaching Acts"; Chapter 17, "Learning to Give Longer Presentations"; Chapter 18, "50-Minute Classes"; Chapter 20, "Explaining by Doing"; Chapter 22, "Observation of Teaching Behaviors"; and Chapter 25, "Overall Observation of Classes."
5. "Nonverbal Communication" (6.7) can be used along with "Observation of the Teacher's Nonverbal Acts" (22.3).
6. "Asking and Answering Questions" (6.8) can be used with "A Reference Guide to Question Structures" (6.9); "A Reference Guide to Question Types" (6.10); "Asking Questions" (3.1.b); Chapter 8, "Leading a Discussion"; and Chapter 24, "Observation of Use of Questions by Teachers and Students."
7. Chapter 7, "Using Audiovisual Aids," can be used along with Chapter 6, "Presenting in Class or Lab," and Chapter 22, "Observation of Teaching Behaviors."
8. Chapter 8, "Leading a Discussion," can be used along with "Discussing" (3.1.c); Chapter 4, "Profiles of Teachers in American Colleges and Universities"; "Asking and Answering Questions" (6.8); Chapter 19, "Leading Discussions"; and Chapter 22, "Observation of Teaching Behaviors."
9. Chapter 9, "Preparing Tests, Grading, and Record Keeping," can be used along with Chapter 2, "Departmental Relations"; Chapter 3, "Profiles of American Students" (especially "Asking Questions" [3.1.b], "Challenging and Disputing" [3.1.d], and "Questioning Grades" [3.2.b]); Chapter 4, "Profiles of Teachers in American Colleges and Universities" (especially "Course Designer" [4.1.a] and "Dealing With Varieties of Students" [4.2.a]); "Announcing a Test" (16.4); and "Returning Tests" (16.6).
10. The various materials and activities that focus on explaining and explanations are found in Chapter 6, "Presenting in Class or Lab"; Chapter 15, "Learning to Give Short Explanations"; Chapter 16, "Giving Mini-Lectures to Practice Particular Teaching Acts"; Chapter 17, "Learning to Give Longer Presentations"; Chapter 18, "50-Minute Classes"; and "Leading a Discussion of an Explanation" (19.4).